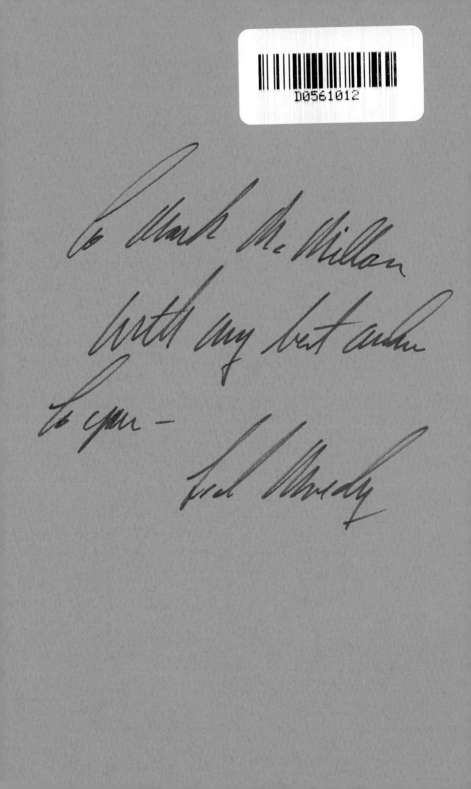

To Mark McMillan
with my best wishes
to you –

Fred Kennedy

# In Critical Condition

## THE CRISIS IN AMERICA'S HEALTH CARE

BY

## Edward M. Kennedy

SIMON AND SCHUSTER

NEW YORK

First printing
SBN 671-21314-8
Library of Congress Catalog Card Number: 72-78542
Designed by Irving Perkins
Manufactured in the United States of America
By H. Wolff, New York, N. Y.


A portion of this book has appeared in
*McCalls Magazine.*

# ACKNOWLEDGMENTS

I am extremely grateful to the leaders in health care and labor, and to the legislative departments of the AFL-CIO, the United Auto Workers, the International Brotherhood of Teamsters, and to the members of the Committee for National Health Insurance, particularly to Max W. Fine, its executive director, for their encouragement and guidance in the development of my basic perspectives on health care. Stanley B. Jones, of my Senate Subcommittee on Health, contributed the major effort in the preparation and compilation of the material, supported by LeRoy G. Goldman, subcommittee staff director, and S. Philip Caper, M.D., also a staff member. My special thanks go to them, as well as to the committee secretaries, Mary M. Martin, Anne M. Hocutt and Janet Mullins.

THIS BOOK IS DEDICATED
TO THE MANY UNSELFISH MEN AND WOMEN
WHOSE TESTIMONY IN THESE PAGES
CLEARLY IDENTIFIES THE CRISIS
IN HEALTH CARE IN AMERICA.

# Contents

10                                    *Contents*

# Introduction

I HAVE personally tasted the tragedy of illness and injuries. In 1964 I survived a disastrous small-plane crash in which my back was broken and in which two other men were killed. I—and my family—suffered through a six-month hospitalization, during which I was immobilized on a striker frame, wondering how disabled I would be and whether my career would end as a result of the injury. My brother Jack returned from World War II with a back injury that threatened to disable him and that plagued him during his Presidency and all his life. We watched him go through several hospitals and wondered what kind of life would be left to him when it was over. We also watched my father struggle through the last seven years of his life with the crippling effects of a stroke. Our family knows only too well the tragedy of illness and injury, and the deep personal value of good health.

I recall my mother's carefully kept records of every childhood illness and every immunization for each of her children. Like millions of American women, she was determined to make sure that her children had the best possible chance she could give them for a healthy life.

These personal experiences fostered my growing interest in health during my ten years in the Senate of the United States.

When my colleagues chose me as chairman of the Senate Sub-committee on Health in January of 1971, I was given an opportunity to study and work to fill our nation's health needs.

I believe most Americans sense that good health is a basic part of a larger dream of opportunity. We know that children who are not given immunizations and regular child care, and indeed anyone troubled and held down by illness or injury, will not have the same opportunity for life, liberty, and the pursuit of happiness as a man who has his health. My family has been fortunate by and large to get health care good enough to give us every opportunity for full and healthy lives. We have also been fortunate to be able to afford that care, for the cost has been terribly high.

Not all Americans, however, have been so fortunate. And all Americans find that health care is taking a bigger and bigger share of their incomes, that they have little assurance of the quality of care they are receiving, and that, regardless of their incomes, they are vulnerable to financial ruin because of health care costs.

Are you aware that all Americans are paying today over 170 percent of the hospital daily service charges they paid in 1960? Do you know that medical costs force Americans of every income level to mortgage their families' future, sell their homes, give up their children's college education, and even declare bankruptcy? Many are hounded by collection agencies hired by hospitals and doctors. Many have their salaries garnisheed; some are sued. Four out of five Americans have health insurance of some kind, but most are surprised when they find out too late that their policy covers much less than they thought, excludes the particular health problem they're faced with, or has lapsed because, for example, they were laid off or changed jobs.

Are you aware that millions of other Americans who are

sick or injured get no help at all from doctors and hospitals? Some are turned away because they can't pay. Some wait for eight hours or more in crowded emergency rooms, only to give up and go home without help. Some live in areas of the country or the city that have been abandoned by doctors. And many, many other Americans have simply given up trying to get care because they know they can't afford it—or they know they'll be insulted or abused by the "charity" care which is the only kind that is offered to them. One out of seven Americans has no health insurance at all because he can't afford it or has a health problem that makes him uninsurable.

Are you aware that the quality of health care Americans receive varies widely, and while some receive the best in the world, many others suffer through unnecessary operations or prolonged illnesses, and some even die because of poor care. Sadly enough, the person who is receiving the care seldom knows how good or how bad it is.

Finally, are you aware that America's $17-billion-a-year health insurance industry takes enormous salaries, commissions and profits out of the premiums you pay, and does little or nothing to control physicians' and hospitals' charges or stimulate them to deliver better health care to Americans? In fact, the insurance industry, by its policies, encourages inefficient health care and all too often turns hospitals and physicians into businessmen first and healers only second.

While chairing health subcommittee* hearings in Wash-

---

* The members of the Senate Health Subcommittee are: Democrats —Edward M. Kennedy, Chairman, Harrison A. Williams, Jr., Gaylord Nelson, Thomas F. Eagleton, Alan Cranston, Harold E. Hughes, Claiborne Pell, Walter F. Mondale; Republicans—Richard S. Schweiker, Jacob K. Javits, Peter H. Dominick, Bob Packwood, Glenn J. Beall, Jr., Robert Taft, Jr.

ington and across the nation, I have heard witness after witness describe his personal disaster in seeking health care, and have heard statistics which show America spending more and more money on health care but falling further and further behind other nations in its level of health.

I was appalled to hear Mrs. Aurora Rodarte describe how she tried unsuccessfully in Los Angeles to get doctors in an emergency room to take her husband's stroke seriously. What happened to him? "He died," she said.

One person after another startled our subcommittee by testifying to harassment by collection agencies after a serious illness. Mr. James Rieger, in Cleveland, described how such an agency took his family's car, stove, refrigerator, television, and everything they were buying on credit to pay $20,000 in doctor and hospital bills. Mr. Rieger had lost his premature child and almost lost his wife when she suffered heart failure while giving birth. Mr. Rieger's family—like dozens of others we heard from—had these disastrous bills piled on top of the great personal tragedy of illness and death.

I was surprised to learn of the power of medical societies in maintaining laws in twenty-two states which restrict physicians from forming new types of group practice to compete with older forms of solo practice.

Miss Angie Roby, a nurse in Des Moines, told a story of terrible institutional callousness. She described how a hospital's utilization review committee forced her invalid brother out of the hospital with no concern for where he would go. The boy's mother and brother had been admitted for psychiatric care, and Miss Roby was forced to canvass scores of nursing homes for a place for her brother.

I was saddened by the story of Mrs. Catherine Calcioli, an elderly widow in West Virginia, who received meager health benefits from five state and federal programs, struggling to figure out what she could claim from each program to live on her income of fifty-six dollars a month. Her doctor wouldn't even help her fill out her insurance claim forms—he doesn't believe in insurance.

Story after story demonstrates people's agony in trying to get a doctor to look at a suffering member of their family. From Senator Harold E. Hughes, former governor of Iowa, to Mr. Gerardo Martinez, a migrant worker in the San Fernando Valley, we heard stories of frantic efforts to get help after hours. As Senator Hughes said, "When that happens to the governor, you know, I wonder what happens to the rest of the people."

I am ashamed to say that these things happen in America, in the richest country in the world. Smaller countries spend smaller amounts on health care than the United States, and they give more health care to their people. In many of these nations, fewer children die than in America, fewer women die in childbirth, and men and women live longer lives on the average. Some say it would be too expensive to provide more health care to Americans, but in the countries our subcommittee visited in 1971—Great Britain, Denmark, Sweden, Israel—this proved to be not true.

I am shocked to find that we in America have created a health care system that can be so callous to human suffering, so intent on high salaries and profits, and so unconcerned for the needs of our people. American families, regardless of income, are offered health care of uncertain quality, at inflated prices, and at a time and in a manner and a place more suited to the convenience and profit of the doctor and the hospital than to the needs of the patient. Our system especially victimizes Americans whose age, health, or low income leaves them less able to fight their way into the health care system. The health care industry seems by its nature to give most freedom and power to the providers of care—and very little to the people. It is an industry in which there is very little incentive to offer services responsive to the people's needs and demands. It is an industry which strongly protects the profit and rights of the provider, but only weakly protects the healing and the rights of the people.

The stories I have heard are deeply personal and human tragedies. Illness and injury have a profound and personal impact on a family. All of us know the suffering of illness and the suffering that goes with watching a friend or one of our children racked with the pains of illness or injury, wondering whether they will recover, wondering whether their lives or careers will be crippled. At such times we grow frantic for help and will do anything to get a doctor or a hospital. At such times also we are deeply grateful for the help we do get, and do not stop to worry about how much it will cost. Unfortunately, that cost can later turn out to be more than we can afford to pay except by mortgaging our family's future.

Even though we are a nation that places a high value on health, we have done very little to insure that quality health care is available to all of us at a price we can afford. We have allowed rural and inner-city areas to be slowly abandoned by doctors. We have allowed hundreds of insurance companies to create thousands of complicated policies that trap Americans in gaps, limitations, and exclusions in coverage, and that offer disastrously low benefits which spell financial disaster for a family when serious illness or injury strikes. We have allowed doctor and hospital charges to skyrocket out of control through wasteful and inefficient practices to the point where more and more Americans are finding it difficult to pay for health care and health insurance. We have also allowed physicians and hospitals to practice with little or no review of the quality of their work, and with few requirements to keep their knowledge up to date or to limit themselves to the areas where they are qualified. In our concern not to infringe on doctors' and hospitals' rights as entrepreneurs, we have allowed them to offer care in ways, at times, in places, and at prices designed more for their convenience and profit than for the good of the American people.

When I say "we have allowed," I mean that the American people have not done anything about it through their government, that the medical societies and hospital associations have done far too little about it, and that the insurance companies have done little or nothing about it.

I believe the time has come in our nation for the people to take action to solve these problems.

I believe good health care should be a right for all Americans. Health is so basic to a man's ability to bring to fruition his opportunities as an American that each of us should guarantee the best possible health care to every American at a cost he can afford. Health care is not a luxury or an optional service we can do without. Every child who is retarded or whose arms or legs remain twisted because his parents could not get care, every family that faces financial disaster because of the cost of illness or is broken by unnecessary suffering or death, is kept from fulfilling the right to life, liberty, and the pursuit of happiness that we cherish in America.

The fact that disease and injury deprive many Americans of the opportunity to fulfill these rights because they were born in the wrong place, or because their families could not pay the price, denies our belief that men are created equal and should have equal opportunity. Disease and injury can strike any of us—it is a matter of good or bad fortune. Disease and injury can leave any of us broken both physically

and financially because we did not get good health care and
paid dearly for what we did get.

We have the knowledge, wealth and ability in America to
assure that every American gets the health care he needs and
is not faced by financial ruin in the process. We can guarantee each other good health care. The question is, do we have
the will to do it? If we have the will, we can assure to each
other lives of greater opportunity and dignity.

I believe Americans increasingly feel we should guarantee
good health care to every American at an affordable cost. I
believe more and more Americans are willing to share the
responsibility of making this guarantee. The Congress reflects
this growing sentiment in its current activities.

In the fall of 1971, the Congress passed a $3.8-billion bill
designed to increase the number of physicians, physicians'
assistants, dentists, nurses, and other health professionals in
the country, as well as to train health personnel to work together in new and better ways of providing health care. This
law also offers incentives to health professionals to enter
medical specialties that are in short supply and areas of the
country that are short of health care.

This law marks a major new federal role in supporting the
education of health professionals and encouraging change in
how and where these professionals practice. An expanded
federal role is also contemplated in bills before the Senate
Health Subcommittee to encourage physicians and other professionals to form prepaid group practices. In these group
practices the patient pays a set yearly fee per person or per
family which covers all basic services, whether in the hospital or in the doctor's office. There is strong reason to believe
that such practices offer efficiencies, economies, and assurances of quality that allow more health care to be given at
less cost. Passage of these bills will again acknowledge a

federal role in guaranteeing that health care is organized and delivered in a way that assures the people of its quality and efficiency.

In addition, the Senate Health Subcommittee in the months ahead will be reviewing some fourteen expiring federal laws which support better planning of health services, research and development on new ways of supplying services, neighborhood health centers, childhood immunizations including rubella, measles, and polio, and a variety of other programs. I am confident that extensions of these laws will acknowledge an expanded federal responsibility for improving the way health care is organized and delivered in America.

There is a second kind of bill before Congress, however, whose implications for health care in America are even more profound. The President, the American Medical Association, the Health Insurance Association of America, and others have submitted proposals to establish a national health insurance. I have introduced such a proposal in the Senate—the Health Security Act, Senate Bill No. 3. Congresswoman Martha W. Griffiths has introduced this same bill in the House of Representatives, H.R. 22. All of these bills, in various ways and to various degrees, attempt to assure Americans better and broader health insurance coverage. These bills involve billions of dollars and imply a much wider federal role in paying for and regulating health care. They differ radically in the comprehensiveness of their coverage, the extent to which they attempt to control the costs and methods of delivering of care, and the role they allow the private health insurance industry.

These bills are currently before the Senate Finance Committee, chaired by Senator Russell B. Long, and the House Ways and Means Committee, chaired by Congressman Wilbur D. Mills. Both committees have held hearings, and both have indicated they will take some action in the area of national health insurance coverage.

I believe that the Health Security Act, which I discuss in the last chapter of this book, is the only bill that will assure every American quality health care at a price he can afford. Unfortunately, congressional action might result in piecemeal efforts that would help a few Americans but further imbalance the health-care system and drive up costs without improving the quality of care. The Health Security Act I am proposing is a bold and comprehensive program. How boldly Congress acts will depend on our willingness to demand good health care for one another, and for all Americans.

I am hopeful that this book will help generate such a willingness in you, the reader.

To this end, I want to share with you the things I have seen, the stories I have heard about health care in the United States during hearings, meetings, and site visits made by the Health Subcommittee in 1971 on the topic "The Health Care Crisis in America." These hearings were held in Washington and in nine cities across the nation and in several European countries. I have organized these stories and experiences around key questions of conscience, the answers to which I believe add up to an answer to the larger question: Should we assure quality health care to every American as a matter of right?

The first eight chapters of the book raise specific questions, offer illustrations of the human problems involved in the question, and offer my thinking and choice of conscience in each case.

1. Should good health care cost an American everything he owns?
2. Should good health care mortgage a family's future?

3. Should Americans be denied good health care because they cannot pay?
4. Should Americans seek out health care or should health care seek out those in need?
5. Should Americans organize their health care or should the health care system organize itself?
6. Should Americans be left to find high-quality care or should the health care system guarantee quality?
7. Should hospitals and doctors be both businessmen and healers?
8. Should health insurance be big business?

Not all of these questions allow yes or no, either/or answers. Not all are objective; my beliefs have no doubt crept into the formulation of both the question and the answer. There are, moreover, many other valid questions that might be raised.

These are questions, however, that all Americans are asking, whether they are the people who use health services, the doctors, dentists, hospital workers and others who provide health services, or the people whose work in government or industry is involved with health services. I was impressed by the words of Dr. Kenneth Platt, president elect of the Colorado Medical Society during our subcommittee field hearings in Denver. We had spent much of the day observing some truly excellent medical care and had then heard testimony from a number of witnesses whose stories illustrated some of our failures to bring this care to all Americans. After hearing these witnesses, Dr. Platt said:

I would like to speak to you for just a few moments both as a concerned professional and as a compassionate human being. The tragedies you have heard here, both personal and socio-economic, are in a sense the tragedy of all of us. The very fact that one such instance could occur in a country as rich and powerful as this is a concern not only to you and me, but to other taxpaying members of this group today.

This kind of sentiment is triggered in all Americans by their day-to-day experiences in giving or getting health care. It forces us to confront the question of whether good health care should be a right.

On the pages that follow, I say some harshly critical things, especially about the health insurance industry and organized medicine. These criticisms are made from my perspective on the gulf between the right to care and our efforts to provide care. Some of the basic business principles espoused by organized medicine and the health insurance industry seem to me to inhibit hospitals, physicians, and other health care providers from developing ways to respond to our society's growing beliefs. In other cases, I cite examples of problems and abuses in our health care system that hospitals, doctors, and others will resent and term exceptional or unrepresentative of the best in care, which is also offered in this country.

My intent is in fact to point out the problem areas, areas where Americans are clearly not getting the best. In some cases this means highlighting a health care problem of all Americans; in other cases it means highlighting the problems of those for whom getting good care is especially difficult. The point is that we are not offering the best that the knowledge, wealth, power, and vision of this nation will allow— that we are offering less than our growing belief in the right to good health care leads us to expect.

I have tried to look at these problems from the point of

view of the people. Although I have tried to reflect the perspective of the hospitals and physicians, and to defend their rights and freedoms (see especially Chapter VIII), I have dwelt most on the problems as they must appear to those who use the health services. I believe deeply that the people have been given less say in the area of health care than in almost any other area of American life. In no other area do they have so little choice or control. In no other area is the provider of services given such total freedom and authority.

We are faced as a nation with some difficult choices of conscience in the months ahead. Our choice will affect our lives very deeply. Physicians, dentists, nurses, and other providers of health care will be most affected by our choices in that not only their health care but also their livelihoods and patterns of work will be affected.

The last chapter of the book describes my basic choices and the extent of government action I feel is necessary to guarantee health care as a right. I hope that the reader is led to feel the urgency of choosing, and that he will make the same choice that I have made. Those who read but do not agree will at least be in a better position to understand and debate my views, which I intend to pursue vigorously in the Congress.

EDWARD M. KENNEDY

*Washington, D.C., 1972*

CHAPTER I

# Sickness and Bankruptcy –
# a Double Disaster

HEALTH care in America is very, very expensive. If an American has a serious accident, heart disease, cancer, complications in childbirth, kidney disease, or any of a long list of other health problems, he may be faced with financial ruin regardless of his income.

Families which are torn by illness have been forced to sell their homes, to sacrifice in a few weeks savings accumulated over years of hard work, to move in with relatives, and to live in near poverty—all to pay the costs of their tragic illness or accident. Most families struggle to pay, to honor their debts, and to adjust their style of life to live on what is left. For some families, this has meant going on welfare.

Other families, faced with the utter hopelessness of paying their health care debts from their salaries, have been forced to declare bankruptcy. They have seen their cars repossessed, their appliances taken—even their stoves and refrigerators. Once bankrupt, they are forced to pay in advance for everything, including health care, because they have no credit.

There is nothing "different" about people faced with these

tragedies. They come from all walks of life, from the poor to the affluent, from all parts of the country, from every race and religion. Illness and accidents are not limited to any group of people; we are all vulnerable. And when any of us is struck by catastrophic illness, he will also assume enormous medical bills. The bills simply go with illness or accident—there is no getting around it.

Of course, bills that will bankrupt one family may be within another family's ability to pay. It depends on how much income and how much health insurance the family has. Unfortunately, when the bills come most Americans are surprised by how much their insurance does not cover. They find there are ceilings on total payments, as well as "deductibles," "copayments," "coinsurance," or "exclusions." In the end, they find that the portion of the bill that they must pay is enormous—large enough to bankrupt many families, force them on welfare, or mortgage their future regardless of their income.

While all families are vulnerable, millions of Americans who are elderly, who are disabled, or who have part-time, seasonal, or low-paying jobs face financial ruin from bills that most American families could take in their stride. Families on fixed or limited income frequently have no insurance protection at all.

Representatives of Legal Aid Societies in West Virginia and Des Moines pointed out that medical expenses are frequent causes of bankruptcy among such Americans. In many states, Medicaid is of little help. In West Virginia, for example, a married couple with an income of a hundred dollars a month is ineligible for Medicaid. Disabled workers who receive Social Security disability payments and workmen's compensation frequently receive just enough to make them ineligible for Medicaid.

The stories that follow were related at public hearings by people from many segments of society—a bank president, an insurance executive, a furniture repairman, a millworker, a retired brewer, a disabled miner, a college professor, and others. These are people who have had illnesses or accidents which can cost one everything he owns. Some of these people received the best medical care this country, and perhaps the world, can offer. Each of them has faced financial ruin, however, trying to pay the costs of this care. Their stories help force us to face the choice of conscience: Should health care cost you everything you own? They force us to consider how greatly we need as Americans to offer better protection to one another against such tragedies.

### A FOOTBALL INJURY

In Nassau County, New York, we heard testimony from Mr. Leonard Kunken and his son Kenneth. Both insisted on being heard despite the seriousness of Kenneth's condition.

Listen to Kenneth's description of what happened to him, and then to Mr. Kunken's description of the financial consequences.

SENATOR KENNEDY: Ken, we appreciate very much your coming out from the Rusk Institute. As you know, this is the Senate Health Subcommittee. We are interested in health legislation, and we have been holding hearings in Washington and now around the country. And, of course, we are interested in the health care needs of the people of this nation. . . .

You are really providing a great service, I think, to this committee and to the Senate, and I think to the American people, in coming and talking with us today, and I want to express my very deep sense of appreciation on behalf of the committee.

KENNETH KUNKEN: Thank you. . . . I got hurt playing in a football game up at Cornell University, and that was October thirty-first. And since I have been hurt I have been paralyzed from the neck down. And that was instantaneous with the injury. It was after a tackle.

Then I had a bone fusion done in my neck about nine days later, and after about a couple of weeks I did get a little return back in my left arm. And I have the use of my shoulders, but very little else. So there is really nothing that I can do for myself now, or for the last twenty-three or so weeks that it has been since I have been hurt.

So what has been happening is I have had aides and attendants and nurses pretty much around the clock that have had to feed and dress me and turn me, say every two hours, to prevent my getting bedsores or to aid circulation. And I have been undergoing a lot of different sorts of therapy hopefully trying to get some movement back if it is possible. And I have been taking different sorts of breathing treatments because I don't have the full use of my chest cavity, and it is really only my diaphragm, I understand, that is working to keep me breathing. . . .

SENATOR KENNEDY: You wanted to be an engineer?

KENNETH KUNKEN: I did at the time. But I understand it may not be feasible for me to go back into engineering with the movement that I have or my ability to move around.

SENATOR KENNEDY: What kind of activity can you undertake now? Can you read?

KENNETH KUNKEN: Well, they are working on a page

turner for me so that I may be able to read. They would have to prop a book onto the page turner and I would be able to work, say, a button with my chin. But as of yet we haven't come up with a device that works well enough to read without getting really frustrated, because the page turner doesn't work all the time and sometimes it turns more than one page, other times doesn't even turn one page. So since I have been injured I have read very little. . . .

SENATOR KENNEDY: Are you looking forward to trying to go back to school sometime in the future?

KENNETH KUNKEN: Yes, I am. But I am really not sure how that is going to work out, though, once I do go back. I understand I will always need an attendant with me for getting dressed, getting around, feeding, one thing or another. I am not even sure what I would like to study now, too. But I would like to go back to school.

SENATOR DOMINICK: Ken, how many people are there in the institute [for Rehabilitative Medicine] with the same type of situation in which they need attendants all the time? Do you have any idea, or are you alone pretty much?

KENNETH KUNKEN: Well, I don't really have any figures, any real numbers. I have yet to see someone there that has as little movement as I do. . . . I know there are people, though, that do have some movement more than I do, but that they still need attendants and they still need to be fed because the movement they have isn't great enough to allow them to do it themselves.

SENATOR DOMINICK: Are they younger people down there with you or are they older people?

KENNETH KUNKEN: Well, they are mostly people right around my age group, I would say. But I know they do have a pediatrics part to the hospital that I haven't seen, so I know that there are a lot of young kids there.

SENATOR DOMINICK: Are these mostly from accident cases, do you know? . . .

KENNETH KUNKEN: A lot of them have been from automobile accidents. A lot of them have been swimming and diving accidents. Those are the two accidents I think I have seen most commonly since I have been there. . . .

MR. LEONARD KUNKEN [Kenneth's father]: First of all, gentlemen, I want to thank you very much for the opportunity . . . to talk before you today. I feel that I do have a message of great import, and since it happened in my family, to me personally, of course, I can speak with authority. . . .

As a result of Kenny having the spinal cord severed on the fourth and fifth vertebrae he is now a quadriplegic. He cannot move anything beyond his neck, his head, and a slight shoulder movement. He has absolutely no function of his arms, his limbs, nor can he perform the normal body functions that we all do every day. . . .

I might say at the outset that it was rather touch and go for the first week, and, of course, the chances of his survival were quite remote. But he was able to pull through as a result of the excellent care that he received by the doctors up in Elmira, where they transferred him after the accident, and subsequently after remaining there for a month he was brought down to South Nassau Community Hospital in Oceanside, which is the local community hospital where we reside. . . .

I think that the medical staff both at South Nassau and also at Arnett Ogden Hospital in Elmira bent over backwards to minimize their bills. But even though they reduced their fees, I can tell you quite frankly, Senators, that as of the moment, which is now five and a half months today since the accident, our medical costs have been somewhere in the neighborhood of forty-odd thousand dollars, and presently are running at the rate of about $6,500 a month or better. I say "or better" because he is presently at the Institute for Rehabilitative Medicine in New York City, which I believe you are familiar with, and the costs there are more or less on an entirely different basis than they were heretofore at the local community hospitals.

Now, how long he will remain at the institute is problematical. The doctors are trying to perform certain rehabilitation procedures which they think may lead toward Kenny resuming a normal life. . . .

Now, unlike most types of catastrophic situations, there is no end to the medical costs involved. And projecting the medical expenditures in Kenny's behalf, I daresay it is going to be a minimum of anywheres from $75,000 to $100,000 a year.

But even on a basis such as this, if you knew once you had reached a certain amount of monies that were to be expended that that would be it, you could say, "Well, this is the problem, we will have to face it." But I don't see how anybody can cope with such a situation as this, because, frankly, it is endless. There is no end in sight, with all the medical bills. . . .

I do have a major medical policy with my company, and, ironically enough, I am in the insurance business. So it is something that I feel I know first hand. I have been in the business going on twenty-five years, and I have sold a great deal of major medical and life insurance during that period. But to my knowledge there is no plan that is being underwritten by any insurance company that in any way would personally cover all of Kenny's medical expenses.

I have a $25,000 policy with my company, which is the maximum coverage that the company would provide, and it wasn't until just the beginning of this month that they added an additional $15,000, making a total of $40,000 coverage in toto, which is the maximum amount that he will ever be able to have for the rest of his life. I have already used up about forty-odd thousand and the chance of him ever being rehabilitated to the point where he would be self-sustaining or physically fit is out of the question. He is ineligible for ever obtaining more health coverage.

We are talking about a young boy of twenty years of age —one moment his whole life in front of him, and the next moment nothing. Now, my son does not want to become a social charge on the community. He had every indication of becoming an engineer, and if not pursuing an engineering career, possibly an actuarial career with my own company. As a matter of fact, he was to have taken the actuarial exam the week after the accident happened. . . .

They [Cornell University] have contributed at the moment some $12,000, which has been exhausted.

Another fund instituted by the university from a special committee also brought forth an additional ten thousand. But, Senators, we are talking about amounts that run into the hundreds of thousands. So these are, if you will pardon the expression, peanuts. They don't amount to anything after all is said and done, because the situation still exists.

On the other hand, because of his age, twenty, he wasn't covered by Social Security even though he did have a Social Security number. . . . True, he is eligible for Medicaid when he reaches the age of twenty-one. But in order to be eligible for Medicaid, as I understand it, he must more or less make himself destitute, . . . he will not be able to have income of more than approximately 180-odd dollars a month and [must] divest himself of any personal assets that he may own over and above $1,600, which in this day and age is absolutely ridiculous.

How do they expect a young man to be able to face society with this particular dilemma and be absolutely destitute and at the mercy of the world?

I think I better stop now. You might have some questions.

SENATOR KENNEDY: What is your reaction to the system of health in this country that not only burdens you with the enormous personal tragedy in terms of your son, but confronts you with financial ruin?

MR. KUNKEN: The local community where I reside, Oceanside, felt they had a personal interest in Kenny, and they went all out to institute a drive, which is currently in effect, whereby from the schoolchildren on up they are running raffles, they are going from door to door and canvassing, they are doing everything humanly possible in order to raise funds to offset Kenny's medical expenses. . . .

I can't expect these people to constantly shoulder my obligation. And let's face it, being realistic, time has a way of making people forget. . . . Now my next step, then, is to divest myself of all my own personal assets and in turn become destitute in order to qualify for the Medicaid system.

. . . I see major medical insurance, individually and in groups. As good as some of the coverage may be that the companies offer, it is meaningless . . . I believe in free enterprise and I don't feel that I am talking out of both sides of my mouth, [but] I don't feel that the insurance companies—I am talking about the private carriers—can actually take care of the health problem that the people are being confronted with in the United States.

And I might say parenthetically, sir, I am not destitute. But by the same token, when you are talking about sums in excess of a hundred-odd thousand dollars it doesn't take very long to become destitute.

SENATOR KENNEDY: Do you know of any insurance policy

by any private company in this country that could meet the kinds of obligations and responsibilities that you have?

MR. KUNKEN: Well, since this accident came about, Senator, I have heard of one or two where they, let's say, have a deductible of the amount of insurance I currently have in force; that is what they commonly call the piggyback. That would be the deductible, and where that leaves off the other commences. But to my knowledge I never had heard of it until this thing became a reality.

SENATOR KENNEDY: You are in the business.

MR. KUNKEN: I am in the business, and I never heard of it.

SENATOR KENNEDY: This kind of tragedy which has affected your family and your son could really happen to anybody, couldn't it?

MR. KUNKEN: After being at the Institute for the past month and a half and seeing young boys, primarily, that are brought in from all parts of the country, and to see the devastating effects, I know now what people mean when they say, "There but for the grace of God go I." Of course, it happens all over the country. And I am just wondering what the average person has been able to do who doesn't have the major medical coverage that I had or some of the so-called benefits that they gave me—which in this instance is still meaningless, because I will have used them all up very shortly. So I don't think that the average person has even as much coverage or as little coverage as I have. . . .

I can only look at [what it was like for] my immediate family—having always been what I thought was a good breadwinner in my own right—to suddenly be confronted with such a situation, of this magnitude. How could a person who . . . didn't have the wherewithal that I have have been able to cope with this? Impossible.

And he is my son. And it doesn't make any difference how bad his situation is, I must protect him. Now, costs at a stage like this are meaningless. You will do everything, because you only have one life.

One of the common sources of injuries in our country is auto accidents. In Denver we heard from the wife of a bank president whose injuries have kept him from work for months, exhausted his savings, left him and his family dependent on his parents—and there is no end in sight.

MRS. GARY BREEZE: Senator Kennedy, Senator Dominick. Gary's accident was approximately two years ago, in July of 1969. He was driving home from work, and there was an automobile accident. It was a fractured vertebra, C6-C7, a spinal-cord injury, multitudinous internal injuries.

He was taken immediately to Lutheran Hospital. He was in intensive care twelve days there. We were told initially that he would probably be in intensive care for at least a month, but because of an infection he was taken out and put in a private room. He was on a special frame, and these things, of course, necessitated a private room. He was in Lutheran Hospital for three months because of the internal injuries, and then he was at Craig Rehabilitation Center for three months. He was a regular outpatient for approximately two months and has been an outpatient periodically since then.

Our bill at Lutheran Hospital was something like $12,000. Now, Gary was in a rather unique position. He had been president of a bank prior to the accident, and he had the job of voting on a particular type of health insurance that he wanted for the personnel. The staff was relatively young, and, of course, we looked at it from that viewpoint. Consequently, he would look at health insurance as maternity insurance for a wife or as insurance for Johnny's broken arm or a skiing accident or something of this sort, so, of course, we had no precedent as far as something like Gary's accident was concerned. We voted on what the bank could afford and what we knew. Our insurance covered a three-month stay in a hospital and then you're out for three months before it will cover any more in-hospital costs as such, so it did cover the entire cost at Lutheran and about two weeks at Craig.

The costs at Craig, we were told the day before we entered, would be $3,000 a month. The doctor would be $350 a month; prostheses, which would mean braces, wheelchairs, tilt boards, things necessitating skin care, would be $5,000, so these things, of course, we had to pay.

Outpatient care is not considered as a part of the cost. We are still, of course, seeing doctors. We have therapists working with us at all times. These are, of course, you know, on our own.

SENATOR KENNEDY: Now, do I understand that during the time that Mr. Breeze was at the hospital, Blue Cross covered those expenses?

MRS. BREEZE: Yes, we paid something like $875. It covered all but that. . . .

SENATOR KENNEDY: And then you went to—

MRS. BREEZE: Craig Rehabilitation Center.

SENATOR KENNEDY: And you had to make a deposit there, did you?

MRS. BREEZE: Yes, $5,000. . . . Before he entered the center.

SENATOR KENNEDY: And was that money used up?

MRS. BREEZE: Yes, it was, sir.

SENATOR KENNEDY: And he was a bank president?

MRS. BREEZE: He was. . . .

SENATOR KENNEDY: Then after leaving Craig he has also endured some medical expenses?

MRS. BREEZE: As I said, his prosthesis costs over the total run would probably go about $5,000. His drug bills run about seventy-five dollars a month; supplies, fifty to seventy-five dollars a month; and this is the major part of the cost. . . .

SENATOR KENNEDY: How long do you expect these expenses to continue?

MRS. BREEZE: There's no end in sight, Senator.

SENATOR KENNEDY: And who pays for that now, the approximately $150 a month you are now charged?

MRS. BREEZE: Well, we are no longer, of course, on hospitalization insurance. The only thing that the hospitalization would cover at this point would be if Gary were back in a hospital.

SENATOR KENNEDY: And can you get any kind of insurance program now?

MRS. BREEZE: No, not now.

SENATOR KENNEDY: Have you tried to?

MRS. BREEZE: Yes. Of course, we are not insurable now.

SENATOR KENNEDY: Why do you say "of course"? Won't the insurance companies provide any kind of health assistance to someone in your situation?

MRS. BREEZE: No, no.

SENATOR KENNEDY: So you are going to have to pay these bills yourselves?

MRS. BREEZE: I haven't found an insurance company that would cover us at this point. . . .

SENATOR KENNEDY: What are your prospects now? Are you going to have to go on welfare in order to survive?

MRS. BREEZE: No. We are fortunate to have parents that have helped us. We would certainly hope that one of these days Gary will be able to go back to work. . . . We have three little children. It's what he is striving so hard for, but we don't know. . . .

SENATOR DOMINICK: The real question is, how do you finance these kinds of things? I don't quite understand the financing at Craig. I understand that Craig Rehabilitation Hospital had been built almost entirely on voluntary contributions. There are people at Craig—which we saw this morning—who I'm sure have the same or perhaps even greater problems than you have and there is still hope that all of these people will be able to go back to work.

MRS. BREEZE: Of course.

SENATOR DOMINICK: Now, I wish you the best. I think this is terrible for you, for the county and for the state. I'm sorry it happened.

A HEART DISEASE VICTIM

The leading cause of death and disability in this country is heart disease. It is an expensive illness, because it usually requires hospitalization and follow-up drugs and visits to the doctor's office. Take, for example, the case of Mr. Patrick Smythe.

MRS. SMYTHE: Two years ago last January [my husband] had heart surgery. For one year previous to that he had suffered numerous heart attacks.

We did not live in Denver then. However, we were recommended two years ago to a doctor in Denver. We came here.

He began the surgery. It was a special kind of surgery with a graft. I can't explain it to you, because I'm not familiar with—

SENATOR KENNEDY: Is that open-heart surgery?

MRS. SMYTHE: Yes. They take arteries and graft them into the heart or something.

Shortly after the heart surgery, while he was still in the hospital and had just been taken out of intensive care, he had to have ulcer surgery. As a matter of fact, he almost bled to death before they decided they would have to chance the operation.

Shortly before the latter part of May he was allowed to go back to our home. He had been in Denver all that time, most of the time in the hospital. After we had gone home and had been home about six weeks, he once again had to come into Denver for more surgery because incisions would not heal.

He then went home, and it was then that we moved to Denver. Mr. Smythe was told he could not go back to work for one year after the surgery, so this means one person earning the living. Our insurance was exhausted completely—we had a $15,000 major-medical policy from Prudential, which had been gone for some time. In the home town where we lived everybody knew the history, everybody is afraid to give this man a job. You know—"What if he has a heart attack while he is working for us? We don't want this man in the place."

We moved to Denver, and we found a kind person that gave him a job. . . . However, the person he works for does not offer medical insurance.

I also work. I work for Coors Porcelain, and they do have a medical plan. I'm not very familiar with what it is—I have just recently gone to work there. But they will not accept him for eleven months thereafter. Each doctor's call, each hospital call, everything that happens to us is out of our own pocket.

Incidentally, our bills were over $30,000. We lost our home. The year he had the surgery, our son was a junior in college. I did work, and through the help of my father we did get him through school. But it has left us at this point with basically nothing.

Mr. Smythe's pay is around $220 a month. This is after taxes. I, after taxes, bring home around ninety dollars a week. Of this we are paying a hundred and fifty dollars on one hospital bill each month. We are paying thirty dollars on another hospital bill. We are paying two different doctors fifty dollars a month, so after this you see how little we have to live on.

Now, I want you to know that I am not condemning the surgeon. I think he's one of the finest. . . . I'm not condemning the hospital, because he got fine care, but, by God, he should have had fine care for what they charged. I mean, truly. I shouldn't have said that one word, but—

SENATOR KENNEDY: No reason why you shouldn't.

MRS. SMYTHE: It is expensive care, $x$ amounts of dollars. There is no such thing as little bills. Everything is not one dollar but hundreds of dollars. . . .

SENATOR KENNEDY: Now you had medical insurance which paid $15,000 of the approximately $30,000 bill, is that right?

MRS. SMYTHE: That's right. Of course, we have our apartment.

SENATOR KENNEDY: How do you live?

MRS. SMYTHE: It's pretty slim. As a matter of fact, I was kind of reluctant to use the gas to come over here today. I have that gauged down as to how I can get to work with $x$

number of gallons, and this has to come out each month.

SENATOR KENNEDY: What about your house?

MRS. SMYTHE: We lost our house. We sold it. We took what we could out of it to pay off some other bills. . . .

SENATOR KENNEDY: How long do you think you will be paying off medical bills?

MRS. SMYTHE: For the rest of my life.

SENATOR KENNEDY: What do you think now of the insurance policy you had?

MRS. SMYTHE: I think our insurance policy wasn't big enough, as I think most American insurance policies aren't big enough, but can most Americans afford a bigger policy? If you go to a $30,000 major medical, the average person may not be able to afford it.

A CANCER VICTIM

Another major and dreaded disease is cancer. According to estimates, almost a million Americans were under treatment for some form of cancer in 1971. In some cases the progress and expense of the disease is spread over years; in others it brings sudden disaster. In all cases, it is terribly expensive.

Mrs. Jean May of Nashville, Tennessee, described the case of a university professor who assisted her as a consultant on a study of health care in Nashville.

MRS. MAY: During the course of the time we were consulting him, he became ill with what eventually was diagnosed as cancer of the brain. The man died at the age of forty-six, leaving his widow with staggering bills. Her estimate was that the total bills amounted to about $20,000. These were people who had status in the community, who had every reason to feel very secure because they were covered by what they thought was an adequate insurance plan until such time as catastrophic illness hit them.

There is an additional irony in this story. About six months before he died, the professor was offered a position in Israel, which was their original home, and the widow feels most strongly about this. Had they lived in the country of their origin, which has a completely different system of medical care, this entire tragic event would have had no financial consequence for her whatsoever, because under the system of medical care in Israel all medical bills would have been paid.

COMPLICATIONS OF CHILDBIRTH

One medical expense that most young couples expect and plan for is pregnancy and childbirth. Not many young couples appreciate, however, the risks of complications in childbirth and pregnancy and the limitations of their insurance coverage. Fortunately, medical science can deal with most of these problems, even though the United States is fourteenth among industrialized nations in infant mortality and fifteenth in maternal mortality. The cost of care, however, is high and many insurance policies do not cover the infant during its first fourteen days of life.

Mr. James Rieger told of his wife's problems in childbirth during our hearing in Cleveland.

MR. RIEGER: Well, I have a wife who was about to have a baby. . . . I had hospitalization insurance through my employer. . . . I work for Joseph Feiss and Company, a clothing manufacturer. . . . While giving birth, my wife had a cardiac arrest—her heart stopped—and they had to perform a tracheotomy to assist her breathing and several electrical shock treatments to restart her heart. Then she caught pneumonia, and her lungs collapsed.

She was in intensive care at the Cleveland Metropolitan Hospital for approximately two months, and the child, who was two months premature, was in the infant intensive care unit for two months. And the total bills came out to about $20,000.

SENATOR KENNEDY: This was for the care that was provided to your wife when she had these complications involved in childbirth and to your premature child in the children's intensive care ward?

MR. RIEGER: Right. They had to put tubes in her chest, and quite a few other things. They put a leader into her heart to register the pressure caused by all the fluids they were giving her, because they had her on I.V.s for a long time.

And all my insurance paid was $350 of it. And there was no way I could pay the rest. We have only been married for a couple of years now, and this was our second child, And, at the time, I had been laid off. There was a trucking strike going on. There was nothing else I could do but go into bankruptcy.

SENATOR KENNEDY: Is your wife covered by an insurance program, too?

MR. RIEGER: No. See, my wife had been working at the same place I was, Joseph Feiss and Company, but when she became pregnant she had to take a leave of absence. . . .

SENATOR KENNEDY: And your child was in the intensive care for how long?

MR. RIEGER: Well, she was six months old when she passed away a month ago. Out of the six months, she spent five months in intensive care.

SENATOR KENNEDY: You have this debt of some $20,000 to the hospital?

MR. RIEGER: Right.

SENATOR KENNEDY: Now, did the hospital try to collect this money?

MR. RIEGER: Yes, they called me up three times before I finally got to my lawyer. . . . I believe the credit department called and said, "Mr. Rieger, you owe us some money. When are you going to come up with it?" . . . I told them I couldn't get $20,000. And the lady on the phone said, "Why don't you go to a finance company and borrow $20,000?"

SENATOR KENNEDY: What did you say when she said that?

MR. RIEGER: I asked her which loan company would give me that much money. I doubt if any would. . . . I told them if they would come down to a reasonable amount that I could possibly handle, I would be more than glad to handle it. Because, like I said, they saved my wife's life and my baby's life. . . .

SENATOR KENNEDY: What do you make a week?

MR. RIEGER: My take-home pay is about $120. . . .

SENATOR KENNEDY: I understand you are going into bankruptcy now?

MR. RIEGER: My bankruptcy petition is already filed. I lost everything, you know.

SENATOR KENNEDY: What do you mean, you lost everything?

MR. RIEGER: Well, I had a car which was—well, it was stolen while she was in the hospital. And I lost the stove, refrigerator, television set. Everything was taken from us since I filed bankruptcy. . . .

SENATOR KENNEDY: As soon as you went into bankruptcy, you lost all the things you had on credit; and most people today, as I understand, are on credit? . . .

MR. RIEGER: Yes. They came right away and took them. I tried calling the bank that I had [financed] the stove and refrigerator and TV through; I explained to them I would like to revive it, but they wouldn't talk to me. What can I do? And the damage this has caused is something I will be feeling probably for quite a few years.

SENATOR KENNEDY: What do you mean by that, now?

MR. RIEGER: Well, as it is, the only way I can buy anything I want or need, no matter how bad a necessity it might be, is by paying cash for it.

SENATOR KENNEDY: That will be hanging over your head probably the rest of your life.

MR. RIEGER: Oh, yes, definitely. They look up your record through some firm, and they say, "He went bankrupt." And then nothing.

SENATOR KENNNEDY: Has this had any impact on your employment?"

MR. RIEGER: I am extremely, extremely lucky that I worked for who I do work for. Because they knew of the trouble I was getting into, and they stood by me all the way, so I was very lucky. . . .

SENATOR KENNEDY: Mr. Rieger, this could happen to anyone, this kind of problem. The complications of childbirth that were involved produced this extraordinary medical bill, $20,000 in four or five months. This could happen to anyone in this country. And, of course, the question I think we as Americans have to ask ourselves is, "Why do we have to have a system which adds such a financial burden to the pain and trauma and sense of loss that you felt in terms of your infant, and the extraordinary kinds of hardships that your wife has been confronted with?"

I think you should be asking us, "Why in this nation of ours don't we have a health system that is more compassionate, more concerned, and more sensitive to these kinds of needs?" That question is long, long overdue.

A CASE OF KIDNEY DISEASE

One relatively rare but particularly tragic health problem is acute or chronic kidney disease. People afflicted with this disease can be treated by dialysis—a mechanical process for purifying the blood. We heard from Americans with this problem all over the country. Dialysis units are in relatively short supply; staff to operate the equipment is in even shorter supply.

In Iowa we heard of a patient in the rural town of Osceola who leaves home at 6 A.M. once each week to travel over 150 miles to Iowa City, spends the day receiving and recovering from dialysis, and travels home to arrive late at night. Dialysis is expensive and is seldom covered by insurance.

In New York City, Mr. John Hoh of the Teamsters' Union brought Mr. Eddie Kaiser to our hearing. Mr. Kaiser had been a member of the union for forty years and currently was retired because of kidney disease.

SENATOR KENNEDY: Tell me just a little bit about yourself, Mr. Kaiser. You have been a member of this union for forty years?

MR. KAISER: Yes, for a long time.

SENATOR KENNEDY: How old are you?

MR. KAISER: I am sixty-three now. . . .

SENATOR KENNEDY: And then how long ago did you become sick?

MR. KAISER: When I went for induction in the Army they held me over for three days and they rejected me because, I assume, something was wrong with my kidneys, because of the tests they took, So after that I went to a kidney specialist and he told me at that time that I did have a kidney condition, but there was nothing to be done at the present time except keep in touch with the medical doctor.

Over a period of twenty years this condition got worse, and at that time I made connection through the Teamsters with a doctor up in Riverdale, New York, and this doctor in Riverdale told me that a doctor over in my borough of Brooklyn was setting up a dialysis unit and that I should get my family doctor to get in touch with this doctor. And after going to that clinic for about six months they told me that further therapy was needed, and when they said further therapy they meant I had to go on a kidney machine.

Now, this was about two years ago. . . . After seeing a psychiatrist, a psychologist, and a social worker, and several other tests to go through, they accepted me in this program.

SENATOR KENNEDY: Why did you have to go through all these other tests?

MR. KAISER: To see if you are mentally able to take the shock that you have this condition, that you may have to go on this machine which requires treatments three times a week, four hours each treatment, and you have to have an assistant, which in my case is my wife, to help out in this program.

SENATOR KENNEDY: Now I understand. I am sure there are a lot of people that don't quite understand dialysis. Do you have to go three times a week—"

MR. KAISER: I have it at home. I have to have the unit at home, and three times a week I have to connect my arterial and venous vessels up with this machine and have the blood run through this purifier and come back into me, and that is the treatment—four hours. Four hours each treatment, three times a week.

SENATOR KENNEDY: Now, if you didn't have this treatment—

MR. KAISER: There would be no other way of keeping me alive.

SENATOR KENNEDY: If this weren't available to you over what period of time? Over, say—

MR. KAISER: Well, it may vary in different people, you know. This condition came on me so slowly that my body became accustomed to the high amount of poison that was in the blood. In other words, I could tolerate more than somebody else who had an acute case. Mine was chronic.

SENATOR KENNEDY: Now, is this procedure costly?

MR. KAISER: It costs just for the supplies alone between five and six thousand dollars a year, and if I didn't have my wife to act as my nurse for three days a week it would cost me about $10,000 a year. And the machine itself, I think, is around $2,500.

SENATOR KENNEDY: And you rent that machine?

MR. KAISER: No, I received the machine from Elmhurst General Hospital. Elmhurst General Hospital gives it to me because of the fact that they are subsidized by the federal government insofar as the machine is concerned. But the city of New York is the party who is paying for the supplies, and due to the financial crisis in the city of New York and the state of New York we have been told by the administrator of the program that we will have to find ways and means of financially paying for this program ourselves. Now, this may take place in two or three months. It may not take place at all. They don't know. I think it is according to the city and the state how much money is supplied, how many funds are available for this. . . .

SENATOR KENNEDY: And now you have had some conversation with the administrator of the hospital.

MR. KAISER: With the administrator. We have 150 people there, and they are all being told the same story. He said that you know what the situation is in regard to the financial crisis in New York, in the state and city of New York, and it may be that . . . this lifesaving equipment is going to be eliminated altogether or cut down to a degree where most patients will have to find ways and means of paying for it themselves, and in fact the new people that come into the program are not being accepted unless they can prove that they are financially able to pay for it.

SENATOR KENNEDY: What do they do?

MR. KAISER: They die. In fact, I heard last night on the television news broadcast that there is a vet over in Vietnam who is trying to raise money because his sister and brother need the machine and they are $20,000 in hock already, and he is trying to raise money in Vietnam. And I heard only a short time ago about a baby who has the same condition and she only has a few months to live because they can't get the money to get her a machine.

SENATOR KENNEDY: Will you be able to get the money together yourself?

MR. KAISER: I would be able to get it for a short time and then I would be finished. I have a few dollars, naturally.

SENATOR KENNEDY: But this will take all your savings?

MR. KAISER: I won't last very long at $10,000 a year.

SENATOR KENNEDY: And if the city withholds funds from the hospital and they don't make these supplies available to you, you are unable to raise these kinds of funds?

MR. KAISER: Oh, I can't. Ten thousand dollars a year? I can't raise that kind of money for any length of time, that's a sure thing. I am retired. I am living on Social Security and a brewery worker's pension.

SENATOR KENNEDY: You are sixty-three, so you wouldn't qualify for Medicare.

MR. KAISER: Not for Medicare or Medicaid. . . .

SENATOR KENNEDY: So if there are no funds available, if those funds are cut off what will happen to you?

MR. KAISER: I suppose I would have to die, that's about all. . . .

SENATOR KENNEDY: Well, Mr. Kaiser, we appreciate very much your coming here today. . . . You are a person of modest means and have been struck down through no cause of your own. With this kind of illness, you are completely dependent for medical costs on some kind of additional help and support. I imagine you thought the group policy would cover most of the kinds of illnesses which you would be affected by, but it doesn't reach this enormously costly program, and the city is cutting back on its budget. The real dilemma that is presented to all Americans is whether we are going to continue to tolerate a health care system that cannot provide the kind of help and assistance which you need. I think that is really what we have to address ourselves to.

AN EMPHYSEMA VICTIM

In West Virginia we heard the stories of many retired and disabled workers paying for health care from their limited disability incomes. All were hard-working men whose injuries or lung disease forced them to retire at an early age. Miss Wilda Hess, with the Legal Aid Society in Preston County, West Virginia, told us of the case of Mr. and Mrs. Denver Jones. As with many of the disabled, this couple is too young to qualify for Medicare and has too much income to qualify for Medicaid.

MISS HESS: There was to be another lady with me today. It was only at the very last moment that we learned that she wouldn't be able to appear. Her name is Mrs. Denver Jones. Denver Jones is in his fifties, I believe. He has been receiving Social Security disability for two years. He has emphysema and the heart problems which result. He is confined to bed. He needs oxygen and various medications all the time. Mrs. Jones is in ill health, also. She has had two spinal fusions and she has to wear a back brace all the time.

Mr. Jones has to have oxygen constantly, and their income is $187.30 from Social Security disability and he receives a pension from the Pipefitters' Local of $59.15. That is a total of $246 and some cents. Last month they had to spend $166 for oxygen and $150 for medication. That is a total of $316 on medical bills alone and an income of $246. This is not talking about rent, food, utilities or anything of that nature.

He has been in and out of the hospital many, many times. There is no hospital insurance. They have tried very, very hard. They have borrowed from finance companies in order to pay the hospital bills, so now they owe not only hospital bills and doctor bills, but four finance companies—they are a lot harder to deal with than the hospitals. They have sold everything they possibly can.

When Mr. Jones is well enough to do anything—he is

always bedridden—he paints. She takes in ironing, which, of course, isn't easy to do in her condition, as you can well imagine.

They had hoped to have someone who could stay with Mr. Jones today, but it has to be someone who understands how to administer the oxygen. Three or four people who had promised didn't turn up in the end. So she is unable to be here. She wanted desperately to testify here today and present this situation.


## MY CONVICTION

*No American in our affluent age should be forced to mortgage everything he owns for health care. Granted that men have always been vulnerable to accidents and diseases which have disastrous effects on their lives and their families; however, in America today these tragedies do not have to also bring financial disaster to a family—not in the richest country in the world. We will never eliminate illness and injury, but we can lighten their financial burden. We are rich enough in America to assure each other that those who are stricken with illness need not suffer financial disaster as a result.*

*Americans have a strong custom of pitching in with charity drives and benefits to help an unfortunate neighbor. A lady in Osceola, Iowa, told how they are collecting trading stamps to obtain a kidney dialysis machine for a member of their community. I believe Americans can do better than this. Americans cannot in good conscience allow a family's future to rest on benefits and trading stamps. As Mr. Leonard Kunken put it, "I can't expect these people to constantly shoulder my obligations. And let's face it, being realistic, time has a way of making people forget. At the moment you might say he [Mr. Kunken's son] is good copy. Tomorrow the situation remains, but other than his immediate family there is nobody going to be there."*

*It is unacceptable that our society should abandon Mr. Kunken to lose everything he owns. Nor can we abandon the others whose stories are on these pages—or the millions like them in our country. As a people, we owe them more support. Moreover, tomorrow it may be you or I who face similar disaster. We need as Americans to find ways to share the risks, and to lighten the financial burden on those unfortunate enough to be stricken. To share the risks, we will have to share the costs. But the costs that would destroy any one of us are small when spread among us all according to our ability to pay. I believe it is worth it. We can do this for one another, and we should.*

# CHAPTER II

# What Price Good Health?

HEALTH care is very, very expensive for all Americans, even those who are not struck with bankrupting expenses.

In recent years, Americans have seen their health care costs rise far more rapidly than the price of food or even the price of construction. We have seen hospital costs rise 170 percent from 1960 to 1970. In the same period, doctors' fees have risen sixty percent. Health insurance premiums have kept pace with these increases.

For the vast majority of Americans, health care is an ever-increasing but necessary item in the budget. In good years it may cost only what is required to pay for health insurance premiums and visits to physicians and dentists for minor problems or checkups. In bad years, however, health care costs can force families to set aside plans for buying homes and sending children to college, or to incur debts that will drain the family's budget for many years to come. For some, chronic health problems or disabilities in the family require a sizable share of the family's income to be devoted to health care year after year. Because of rising costs, even routine operations or the delivery of a baby have become major expenses that set back a family's budget for years. As prices rise, we become more and more vulnerable to expenses that cause serious disruption in our family life.

Americans have every right to ask whether health care must cost a family so much of its future. We have a right to ask why hospital, physician, and other charges can't be kept down, and why health insurance must leave families with more to pay than they expected, and many families with bills that literally mortgage their future.

The fact is that health insurance coverages in America are riddled with holes, and they all add up to the same thing for American families: less protection than they think they have and more expense than they can afford. Every story of financial hardship I have heard involves a failure of insurance coverage.

Ideally, health insurance helps to distribute the cost of serious illness or injury among many families in order to lighten the burden on the unfortunate family that is struck with such costs. Ideally, by sharing the risks in this way, we eliminate the impact of sheer "luck"—a family doesn't get wiped out financially just because it is unlucky enough to suffer serious illness.

Unfortunately, insurance in America has not lived up to its ideal. Rising premiums have put adequate insurance beyond the reach of millions of Americans. Millions more buy policies with exclusions, limitations, deductibles and features which lower the policy's value in order to get the premium low enough to afford. Indeed, millions buy health insurance that is not worth the paper it is written on—where the lion's share of the premium payments go for the salesman's commission.

How good our insurance is and consequently how much our family will pay for health care, still boils down to luck.

It depends on whether you work for a company which offers a group plan or not. Some companies offer none.

It depends on how broad and comprehensive the group plan is. Some plans pay a good share of the costs; some pay next to nothing.

If you don't work for such a company, or are self-employed, it depends on whether you belong to some organization that can get group coverage and rates.

In any case, it depends on how much protection you—and others like you in the group—can afford. If you can't afford much, you run a bigger risk of being wiped out by the cost of illness.

If you can't join a group plan, you find it twice as expensive to get insurance, and probably buy only half as much or none at all. You will find that the cost depends on your line of work, the size of your family, where you live, and other factors.

It even depends on how smart you are, how hungry the insurance salesman is, and which insurance company happens to get to you first.

Finally, how much your family will pay for health care depends on whether you are between jobs, in a "waiting period" for coverage, laid off, on maternity leave, or in any of a dozen other situations which may exclude you from coverage when a particular illness strikes.

To top it all off, insurance coverages are so complex that most Americans do not know how good their plans are. We don't know how to judge one against the other and choose the best for our needs. It again comes down to luck.

Regardless of their income, most Americans work to pay off their health care bills, even if it means regular payments and sacrifices for years to come. It is hard for these families to testify at hearings—their stories are less dramatic than those who are bankrupted by the costs of care or who are turned away because they cannot pay. Also, there is a matter of pride which keeps Americans from describing their hardships and sacrifices.

The stories that follow are examples of families who have been unlucky. They were willing to describe their experience in the interest of calling attention to this problem.

### A FURNITURE REPAIRMAN WITH A PRIVATE HEALTH INSURANCE POLICY

One might think that for almost $500 a year a family could buy insurance that covered a problem with a newborn infant. The family in this story, with an income of $7,000 a year, could hardly afford to pay much more than $500 a year for hospitalization alone. But private policies are expensive, and many families, like the De Witt family of Denver, do not know their policies' limitations until they are hit with the charges. Mrs. De Witt and Dr. Butterfield, the director of the newborn center where Mrs. De Witt's child was treated, described to us the bills the De Witts faced because their policy paid limited maternity benefits and excluded complications in the first fifteen days of a child's life. Such complications occur in five percent of newborn children, and in Dr. Butterfield's experience thirty percent of all policies exclude them.

MRS. DE WITT: I live in southwest Denver, in Brentwood. We have had insurance with our company for seven years now and thought we were pretty well covered. But . . . when we found out we were having twins, which was six weeks before they were born, we discovered that we were not covered for the first fifteen days in the hospital. Then one of our babies, unfortunately, was born with a ruptured bowel and has been in the children's hospital for the last month—and we discovered we had no coverage.

SENATOR KENNEDY: What do you mean?

MRS. DE WITT: We found that newborns are completely uncovered for the first fifteen days on our policy. Well, this was kind of bad, because it was a critical time for Debbie. She has had surgery twice, and we wound up with a bill of $5,000. Our hospital insurance has been kind enough to provide something like $700 for the whole thing, so it's been all but pretty much useless.

SENATOR KENNEDY: How long have you had the insurance policy?

MRS. DE WITT: Well, before I was married I had it for three years, and then we have had it seven years as a family policy, so I have been with Prudential for ten years now. . . .

SENATOR KENNEDY: And it excludes the first fifteen days of life. I guess this is a pretty common practice, is it?

MRS. DE WITT: Well, apparently so, because I know I thought that we were the only ones caught by it, but I have run into many parents up there in the last month that have the same difficulty.

SENATOR KENNEDY: Why do you think the insurance companies do that?

MRS. DE WITT: Well, I think it's a pretty handy way to get the premiums and get out of the dangerous part of a new baby. This pretty well fixes them up, because if the baby is going to be sick when it's born this is the bill that's going to be big, and usually it's over by fifteen days and the companies get off pretty well.

SENATOR KENNEDY: How many children do you have?

MRS. DE WITT: We have seven children at home now— well, when we get Debbie home.

SENATOR KENNEDY: And your husband is a furniture repairman?

MRS. DE WITT: Yes, he subcontracts for May–D. and F. He does touch-up work.

SENATOR KENNEDY: How are you paying the bill?

MRS. DE WITT: We haven't quite figured it out yet. I guess we will have to go on payments.

SENATOR KENNEDY: What's your husband's take-home pay?

MRS. DE WITT: It varies with the work that he does. He usually works by the piece. There have been months when we have maybe made three or four hundred dollars and other months we have made eight hundred.

SENATOR KENNEDY: But you are going to have to pay at least some of that, is that right?

MRS. DE WITT: Oh, yes.

SENATOR DOMINICK: Now, on the assumption, then, that nothing happens to them the first fifteen days, I gather the insurance covers the hospitalization during that period?

MRS. DE WITT: Yes. The maternity benefits will pay $250, which, up until this year, has been sufficient. We haven't had any children for four years. This child wasn't really planned, but when we found out we were going to have more, we started saving. The insurance didn't cover anything like the full maternity bill. We still had to pay a balance of $214 just on the maternity bill. . . . We are paying thirty-eight dollars a month for this policy, and we couldn't afford to have it increased to cover the hospital costs as they went up. . . .

SENATOR KENNEDY: Let me ask Dr. Butterfield: Are you affiliated with the hospital?

DR. BUTTERFIELD: Yes, I'm the acting medical director.

SENATOR KENNEDY: Is Mrs. De Witt's situation unusual? How frequently does this kind of situation occur?

DR. BUTTERFIELD: I'm also the director of the newborn center into which this child came for help, and we find that the insurance policy exclusion of the newborn during the first fourteen or fifteen days of life is not uncommon. In fact, we did a study recently and found that about thirty percent of employer's policies had the fourteen-day exclusion. So the newborn, in fact, is a forgotten American in a sense. . . .

SENATOR KENNEDY: How frequently do you find bills of a thousand dollars?

DR. BUTTERFIELD: In our experience, of all infants that have problems that need center-type care in the special unit, approximately half would have bills in excess of a thousand dollars.

SENATOR KENNEDY: How frequently do infants develop complications which bring about medical bills like this?

DR. BUTTERFIELD: I think it's a safe statement to say that about five percent of all children born require some form of intensive care. That's a guess.

SENATOR KENNEDY: They wouldn't be covered by the general kind of insurance policy that Mrs. De Witt has?

DR. BUTTERFIELD: Correct.


### A SCHOOLTEACHER ON MATERNITY LEAVE

One of our witnesses, Mrs. Moore of New York, found that when she took maternity leave from her work she also lost her insurance coverage.

MRS. MOORE: I am kind of part of the depressed middle class. I recently took leave from the New York City Board of Education and went on maternity leave. At the time that I left I was told that I had health insurance, as all New York City employees do. And on February tenth I received a letter from Blue Cross/Blue Shield that said I was not covered. However, for five years while I was teaching, a premium was paid.

During this period I had a Caesarean delivery and eight days in the hospital, a bill which comes to about $2,000. Also, our infant son had to undergo surgery. He was in the hospital for one day for the surgery, and we have a bill of $800 for the surgery and the stay of one day.

We have not heard from Blue Cross/Blue Shield as far as our case goes, except that they refused to pay any of our bills.

SENATOR KENNEDY: Do I understand you correctly that you said it was $800 for one day? . . .

MRS. MOORE: Well, there is a $350 surgeon's fee. There is an anesthesiologist to pay. So for twenty-four hours we would have about $800 in bills to pay, for minor surgery really.

SENATOR KENNEDY: What kind of insurance— You don't have any?

MRS. MOORE: Well, I assumed that I had Blue Shield/Blue Cross major medical. However, their records show that we do not. And the city's records show that we do. There is a discrepancy. But at this point I am being billed for $800 for [my son's] surgery and for $2,000 for the birth and [earlier] stay in the hospital for the child.

I find it kind of incredible. I am in the middle. I was a professional and I worked and I paid my insurance, and now I am liable for let's say $2,800 in medical bills.

We were in London on a holiday two years ago and we had the misfortune that my husband had to have an appendectomy. He was hospitalized for three weeks in London and we did not pay a penny. It was a tragic thing to happen, but we were not doubly liable for this misfortune.

SENATOR KENNEDY: What do you mean, you didn't pay a penny? Did he go to a hospital over there?

MRS. MOORE: He went to a hospital.

SENATOR KENNEDY: Get operated on?

MRS. MOORE: Wonderful care. They did emergency surgery. They have the National Health Act, very similar to what you are proposing. Everyone pays for the National Health.

SENATOR KENNEDY: Did he have laboratory fees?

MRS. MOORE: No fees at all. Absolutely none at all.

SENATOR KENNEDY: No deductibles?

MRS. MOORE: Nothing.

SENATOR KENNEDY: Coinsurance?

MRS. MOORE: Completely covered.

SENATOR KENNEDY: Paperwork?

MRS. MOORE: Nothing. Absolutely nothing. I kind of wonder why it is [that] in a country this wealthy one has to be liable for one's health. It is a double indemnity. I mean it just doesn't work at all. There is no logic to this.

My case may be straightened out, but why is it that the middle-class person, the one who works, also has to worry about Blue Cross and Blue Shield and very high insurance rates and really shudders at the idea of getting sick? The worst thing that could happen to you in America is to get sick, because then you have to pay your doctors, you lose your salary, and you really pay off for the rest of your life.

I had one day's stay and an $800 bill. What happens with someone who is chronically ill?

AN INSURANCE EXECUTIVE WHO COULDN'T GET
COVERAGE FOR HIS WIFE

Even those with higher incomes can have their family finances shattered if they are caught in an insurance loophole. You would think an attorney and executive in an insurance company would be able to avoid getting caught in this. Mr. Sumner Cotton of Los Angeles was caught in such a situation, however, because he could not get coverage for his wife when he left a company with a group plan and applied for private coverage.

SENATOR KENNEDY: You work for an insurance company, is that right?

MR. SUMNER COTTON: I no longer do. I have been in the insurance business about twelve years. So I know the insurance industry quite well. . . .

Just last year, my wife felt kind of ill. She was in and out of the hospital, I guess, five, six times. Had diagnostic studies done. At that time I did have group insurance, so it was marvelous. But they could find nothing specifically wrong with her. She kept complaining of some discomfort, some illness, but they couldn't come up with any particular diagnosis. . . .

Anyway, she obviously had several claims, which were submitted to the private insurance carrier, the group carrier. Nineteen sixty-nine went by relatively well. And in June of 1970, while she was visiting back East, she was stricken with an aneurysm in the anterior-lobe section of the brain.

When I left employment in the insurance industry as an insurance executive I tried to convert the group coverage to some meaningful private coverage, and despite having known a number of good underwriters, it was impossible for me to obtain any meaningful coverage for her. The basis for that was that she had lodged claims five or six times in the preceding year. They said to me—now, this is the personal kind of conversation I had with these gentlemen—"Wait a couple of years, old friend, and if she has had no further claims and she is in good health, why, we will get her some health insurance."

Well, that's great, except before that period she came down with the aneurysm and at that point was not only uninsurable, she was not insured. There was no insurance available on the street, with Blue Cross or what-have-you. No one. Obviously, the financial burden that that event posed was quite substantial.

SENATOR KENNEDY: Now, as I understand, then, you did have some insurance and, as a matter of fact, even worked for an insurance company for ten to twelve years, and when you took another job you lost your health insurance. Is that correct?

MR. COTTON: Well, the group insurance—you can convert a portion of it, but you can't convert the meaningful portion of it. . . .

SENATOR KENNEDY: But your wife was sick during this time, and you were trying to get some other insurance and were unable to do so?

MR. COTTON: Well, she was sick and she wasn't. They couldn't pinpoint what was wrong with her. . . . Insurance companies don't like to buy claims.

SENATOR KENNEDY: Why not?

MR. COTTON: It hurts their profit.

SENATOR KENNEDY: So she was hospitalized and you got the bills. . . . How much was the bill?

MR. COTTON: Oh, the total bill was in excess of thirteen thousand dollars.

SENATOR KENNEDY: Thirteen thousand dollars? And how much of that thirteen thousand was covered by any insurance that you had?

MR. COTTON: Zero. . . .

SENATOR KENNEDY: Are you going to try and pay that off now?

MR. COTTON: Attempting to.

SENATOR KENNEDY: What do you think of the health system that provides not only the pain, hardship, and suffering which you have experienced, and which your wife has experienced, but also the financial indebtedness?

MR. COTTON: We have a problem, number one, with the soaring hospital costs that you have outlined here on the platform, which is obviously true. The second and third problems, really, relate to the private insurance industry. The third problem is relative to the people whom they employ to market these products. There is a great deal of misrepresentation. There is a great deal of half-truths, if you will. And X buys a policy and X thinks he has y and he doesn't have y at all. He has something less, in most cases.

It is unfortunate that the industry itself, and I say this having been in the industry, hasn't really taken up the cudgel, taken up the challenge and really gone forward to the degree that they could. The industry is not known for its progressive nature, either in marketing products or in terms of management techniques.

SENATOR KENNEDY: They do pretty well in profits, don't they? I mean, you look around the skyline and you see new buildings—

MR. COTTON: Well, you have to distinguish between those companies which are stock companies and those which are not stock companies. The stock companies have stockholders and have profits. The nonstock companies are responsible to themselves. It is almost a self-indulgent, self-sustaining kind of management.

SENATOR KENNEDY: Are you on the verge of bankruptcy?

MR. COTTON: Oh, I suppose if I were pushed into a corner right now, I would have no choice.

A FACTORY WORKER WITH A GROUP POLICY

Kidney dialysis is expensive and is seldom fully covered by insurance. The story of Mr. Ralph Tresky is not uncommon.

MR. TRESKY: I live in Garfield Heights [Ohio]. I am here because my wife came down with kidney trouble, kidney failure, in 1969. As far as the doctor in the hospital, everything was fine; it's just that the cost was so great that my insurance didn't cover it all.

Being dialyzed in a hospital is very expensive, and much of the cost is not covered by insurance. My insurance was what is called a basic Blue Cross plan, and I had a $450 surgical benefit. Well, the wife had three operations, so the other two, I had to pay for those myself. But right now I still have an outstanding bill at the hospital for $5,200.

Now, with kidney patients that go home, you have to have a home dialysis machine. Well, the machine itself costs $3,685, an artificial kidney is another $800, you have a blood pump which costs $645, a Hepburn pump $245. The cost is tremendous. Now, the cost for the patient to be dialyzed at home would run you on the average of $250 a month for supplies—blood tubing, concentrate, and so forth. If it wasn't for the man that I work for and the company that I work for — The men in the local had gone out to different locals and collected money, and sold raffle tickets, and they collected over $7,000 to help me purchase the machine so that I could take my wife home. And I had my wife home for about a year and a half, and I can say unfortunately my wife passed away on April the third of a heart attack.

We are in the process right now of setting up a community dialysis center in the city of Cleveland, and my machine will be donated to this community kidney dialysis center. Now, the reason we are trying to get this set up is for people who cannot afford to go to the hospitals to be dialyzed. To be dialyzed in the hospital it costs roughly $10,000 to $15,000 a year. Some insurance plans will cover you for three years in the hospital, but after that what are you going to do, go home and die? They don't cover you any further, people cannot afford to go to the hospital to be dialyzed. That is the reason we are trying to get this center set up—for people who cannot afford to go to the hospital and be dialyzed.

SENATOR KENNEDY: Where do you work

MR. TRESKY: Van Dorn Company.

SENATOR KENNEDY: And did you have a health program in your company?

MR. TRESKY: Well, we have the insurance, yes, hospitalization insurance.

SENATOR KENNEDY: And how much did that cover?

MR. TRESKY: It did not cover the doctor's fees. It covered the rooms. . . . But, like I say, it did not cover for dialyzing.

SENATOR KENNEDY: You have a bill of $5,200?

MR. TRESKY: Right.

SENATOR KENNEDY: There is no way in the world that you could have prevented, that you know about, prevented your wife from having this difficulty?

MR. TRESKY: No, sir, no way in the world. . . . She had strep throat, and that is where the trouble settled.

SENATOR KENNEDY: How old was she when she had the strep throat?

MR. TRESKY: Roughly thirty-two years old. . . .

SENATOR KENNEDY: What is your take-home pay?

MR. TRESKY: Roughly $140 a week.

SENATOR KENNEDY: Do you have other members in your family? Do you have children?

MR. TRESKY: I have two children.

SENATOR KENNEDY: You were trying to provide for those children, provide for their care and their housing and their education and clothing and food and shelter, and also trying to meet the other health needs of your wife, is that right?

MR. TRESKY: Yes, sir.

SENATOR KENNEDY: And you got to the point where you were dependent for your wife's existence on the goodwill of the people where you worked? And with all of this, on top of the heartache, the suffering, you have a bill now of $5,200!

A HOSPITAL WORKER WHOSE POLICY WAS CANCELED

Sometimes insurance salesmen are more concerned with the sale than with the family. After being misled about converting their group coverage to a private policy, the Mapes family faced a more serious problem. In their case, the new insurer canceled their insurance because of a "preexisting condition" that even the parents didn't know about. Legally, the insurance salesman and his company were within their rights; nevertheless, a family is now faced with crippling life-long payments for treatment of an asthmatic condition when they thought they were protected. Mrs. David Mapes of Los Angeles told this story:

MRS. MAPES: I live alone with my three children, and one of them is an asthmatic child, and nearly every year of his life he must be hospitalized for, usually, double lumbar pneumonia.

We had been covered by group medical insurance since birth. But my husband left the company that he was with in order to buy his own business, so he had an insurance agent writing up the package deal for all of the insurance that you need when you go into business, and the man didn't write for the company that provided the coverage in the past. So he said, "Well, no problem. I will just write you a new policy."

And we didn't really understand that our child had asthma. He had had a cold with a bronchial involvement about a month before, and the doctor had said to me kind of in passing, "Let's treat him as if he had asthma, because maybe he has had too many colds, and if we watch the things that he could be allergic to, he might not have so many colds." He wrote "Acute asthma" in the record, and I didn't know it.

A month later we were in the hospital with him with pneumonia, and I went to a pediatrician, who diagnosed him as an asthmatic child. He was in the hospital again about two weeks after that, and about halfway through the second hospitalization the insurance company notified us that we were being dropped, the whole family was being dropped, because we had tried to defraud them.

SENATOR KENNEDY: Tried to what?

MRS. MAPES: Defraud them by denying that he had a pre-existing condition.

SENATOR KENNEDY: The company said that?

MRS. MAPES: Yes. And we threatened to write to the insurance commissioner, and all those things people do. But, you know, we didn't do too much about it. And we went back to the doctor and he said, yes, they came and photographed his records And, "Well, I didn't tell you that he had acute asthma, but you know, that's the way it goes. I can't lie." So we were left with several hundred dollars, I think close to about a thousand, in debt.

We had been a middle-class-type family who believed in yearly checkups and trips to the dentist, but from that point on everything just deteriorated. Our economic situation and our level of health care deteriorated. It was, as I said, our first year in business, and we had gone into debt. We had a precarious financial situation. My husband lost the business. We couldn't pay the taxes on our house, so we had to become renters, and still are. Of course, there were medical, pharmacy and dental bills for other members of the family.

We started a desensitization program after that first hospitalization for the asthmatic child, and that had to be stopped because we got up to around $400 with the pediatrician and he said, "Well, that's tough, but I have done all I can." We didn't make appointments for other needs we had because I couldn't offer payment, and that is definitely a condition for getting an appointment in some doctors' offices.

SENATOR KENNEDY: Now, just go back a little bit, you were covered by Blue Cross and you would still have been covered if you had been able to continue that policy. Is that correct?

MRS. MAPES: Yes. Yes.

SENATOR KENNEDY: But then because you got a new

policy, you were not covered and ran up all of these bills—
your husband changed jobs, and you weren't covered, and
you ran up a good amount of medical bills. What was the
amount, approximately?

MRS. MAPES: Oh, I think $1,500. . . . Which has never
been paid, because since then we had just a general deterio-
ration of our home life, and now it is all mine to take care of.
I am not with my husband now. And I think a lot of our
problem was psychological, because you sort of lose your
dignity when you lose your money, some way or another. . . .

I feel angry because I am working to the limits of my capacity to improve my potential so that my kids don't feel like
poor kids. Sometimes it seems like a losing battle, because
the odds are stacked against people unless they have a large
reserve of money or unless they have the right connections.
I think most of the billions of dollars spent on the highly
sophisticated technological advances are not filtering down
to the average people. Unless you can go long distances or
unless you have a doctor who puts you in the University
Hospital, you really don't get to take advantage of space-age
medicine. Most people are too busy paying their bills for sore
throats and broken arms.

Before we had medical coverage one of the children fell
out of bed and broke her collarbone. It only means a harness
for six weeks, really. There is nothing to do for a broken
collarbone. And it costs $150 because of the X rays. And it
took me a long time to pay it. I had more than one letter from
a collection agency. This is just before I went into Medi-Cal.
The insurance policy I had at that time was like two different
coverages. So I decided to take my children to the hospital
all at one time just for a routine checkup, even when they
were not sick, and I got a bill that I would have trouble paying even when employed. So I only take them when they are

sick, and I wait a while to make sure they are really sick. That's a dangerous game to play. I know a lot of mothers who do it, though. And I think there are times when my son would not have been to the hospital if I had gone in to see the doctor when he had a cold.

A WOMAN WITH NO INSURANCE AT ALL

Some illnesses not only make it difficult to hold down a job, but make it impossible to obtain insurance. In addition, such illnesses may mean regular and sizable expenses over a long period of time.

Grace Bartlett of West Virginia described her costly experience with Addison's disease and her inability to get any insurance at all. Her story should end with a question. How can anyone pay fifty dollars a month on a monthly income of $125?

MISS BARTLETT: Twenty years ago, it was determined that I had borderline Addison's disease. At that time, of course, I quit work. I was not able to go on as I should, but I come from a middle-class family and my family was able to take care of the expenses at that time that were connected with the problem.

Eight years ago my father retired, and I felt then that I was compelled to apply for Social Security disability, which I did, and I have received it. This amounts to about $125 a month. I went through my records, and last year my medicine alone, just maintenance dosages, cost me fifty dollars a month. I had hospitalization last May for three weeks, which cost me $2,100. It is very easy to see that you cannot pay these kinds of expenses and still use what you have. With the death of my father, our income will be much lower yet than it is. I am single and I live at home.

I have been so fortunate that they have been able to at least make payments on hospital bills. But today I feel over-whelmed because I know that the income is much less than it would have been before and so you wonder what you should do.

Two of my brothers are associated with the medical field. I have had advice from both of them. I have a Baker's cyst behind both knees, and one of them is cutting off circulation into the foot. They said I must get this taken care of im-mediately. But believe me, when you have these kinds of ex-penses and you honestly hope to meet them all, you think many times before you go to a doctor or you do anything unnecessary.

My father's expenses were something terrific. He was in West Penn Hospital in Pittsburgh for fifteen days. This ran $68 a day. No middle-class family can reasonably expect to pay the difference there. He went to my brother's home and took treatments there for six weeks following that. . . .

So I strongly feel that somewhere, somehow, we are going to have to find some way we can reach all the people with adequate health care.

SENATOR KENNEDY: Do you have any insurance at all?

MISS BARTLETT: None at all. When I first got sick twenty years ago, health insurance was not this prevalent, and the minute that they diagnosed my condition as being a border-line Addison problem, I was refused time and time again hospitalization insurance. . . .

I have had several contacts with insurance companies. My brother-in-law is an official with Prudential Insurance. They have told me time and time again, "Do not make an application. You may get well enough someday. If you have been turned down once, then you will not be acceptable for insurance. So do not make an application. Make an inquiry, but not an application, because once you do, it is on the record and you will no longer be considered at any time."

SENATOR RANDOLPH: Senator Kennedy, I want to be very careful in my comment, but I have recently made a speech on this subject in West Virginia. I believe there is an unconscionable gap in the insurance coverage by private firms. I believe there is a lack of comprehensive coverage that we must have.

## MY CONVICTION

*No family in America should have to mortgage its future because of misfortunes of illness or accident. How much health care Americans get should depend not on how much they can afford but on how much they need.*

*Adequate health care is too basic to a family's opportunity to hinge on good luck. Luck often places the highest expenses on those of us who are most vulnerable, and in the high-priced field of health care every American family is vulnerable. It is in every American's best interest to share the risks of health care cost, and it is every American's responsibility to contribute to the costs of care.*

*I believe we should take actions to guarantee comprehensive health insurance to all Americans and to assure that health care is available at a cost any American can afford. In my judgment, the best means of doing this is to establish a broad federal insurance program for all Americans which collects premiums through taxes and pays the costs of the vast majority of our health care.*

CHAPTER III

# No Money, No Medical Care

M ANY Americans who can and do pay their health care
bills do not get adequate health care. One reason they
do not is that their concern over what it will cost discourages
them from going to the doctor. They can pay their bills, but,
because the bills are so high, they want as few as possible.
So they stay home or wait until they know it is serious.

This awareness of the expense of health care is sometimes
called "cost-consciousness." I recall one elderly man in New
York City working to pay a $2,201 nursing-home bill. He
said, "I have worked all my life, I have supported and I can
still support myself. . . . Tell the Senators the bill must be
paid. I don't sleep nights. I received the treatment."

This kind of cost-consciousness may prevent some people
from using health care when they don't really need it. However, it discourages many, many people from using health
care when they *do* need it. It discourages people from getting
checkups and routine preventive care—until an illness or
injury has reached the point where the need for help is clear-
cut. Unfortunately, by this time the problem is sometimes

more difficult and costly to treat and takes more of the physician's and hospital's time and resources.

Occasionally insurance deductibles and copayments are defended as assuring that people will remain cost-conscious and not misuse health services. Some argue that if a man has to pay the first hundred dollars and a percentage of all the rest, he is less likely to use health services that he doesn't really need. Unfortunately, the result of these deductibles is also to simply keep those with low incomes from getting any care at all—and to cause even bill-conscious middle-class families to delay when good health care would indicate they should receive medical attention.

In all of my conversations, I have found no one who is favorable to increasing the patient's cost-consciousness except some insurance companies and federal bureaucrats interested in saving money. If a man does not get the health care he needs, it certainly saves money in the short run, though it may mean sacrificing his health. That hardly seems worth it.

Dr. George Himmler, president of the Medical Society of the State of New York, testified in our hearing there:

I don't favor deductibles and coinsurance, for a variety of reasons. I don't think they are good for patients. Obviously, if they need care and can't scratch up the deductible or co-insurance, this is bad for them. And even if it were considered as an insurance mechanism to cut down on utilization, I think even as an insurance mechanism it is not valid and it keeps people from getting health care very often when they need it.

Dr. William Weil, a pediatrician and chairman of the Department of Human Development at Michigan State University, testified to the Health Subcommittee about the many health problems of children. Failure to seek treatment for children can be attributed at least in part to their parents' concern over how much the treatment would cost—even among middle-class families.

DR. WEIL: So there is a great group of people in the middle-income level who are being hurt today by medical care costs or whose children are not getting the kind of care that they ought to, and we see this repeatedly—little incidents like a family that has a child with a little fever, and the question is to call the doctor or not. Well, they just had filled out their various tax forms and they had the rent due, and they know if they call the physician then and they have to bring the children down, this is nine or seven dollars or something, so, "Well, it is just a 102 temperature, let's forget it, maybe it will go away." So this is postponed, and the next day the same kind of decision is made. At some point as this child is developing meningitis they will contact medical care, but it may be just a little longer than it would have been.

I don't think there is one of us who works in hospitals who does not feel, "If they had only come into a medical system a day earlier, twelve hours earlier, two days earlier, the end result might be different."

I am certain that there are financial restraints in any family that delay these kinds of decisions. . . .

SENATOR KENNEDY: You hear frequently from those who believe in the deductibles that, well, if we don't have that ten-dollar or eight-dollar problem facing that parent, they are just going to come down and abuse the devil out of the system and waste a lot of doctors' time. What is your reaction?

DR. WEIL: At least my experience in this has been that that does not occur. I have had the opportunity over the years to provide health care to many people on an essentially free basis because they were medical students or professional colleagues, and so on, and I work entirely with the families— not with the physician, but with his wife and their children— and, as professional courtesy, we never charged these families, so they had essentially unlimited access. I saw these families regularly for preventive care, maintenance of health care, and I never felt abused. When they had a problem or a question, I was available, and I enjoyed it, and I think the illness record of these families was such that it was less than in the general fee-for-services situation.

Dr. Lowell E. Bellin of New York City made the same point in response to my question "Who causes the over-utilization?"

DR. BELLIN: The primary source of over-utilization is the professional, not the patient. I know very often the statement is made, and with very slight justification, that there are patients who go from doctor to doctor wasting time—patients who go from optometrist to optometrist collecting glasses, patients who go from dentist to dentist collecting false teeth and presumably putting them in a drawer. I would say there are some patients like that, but from the standpoint of actual expenditure, any kind of a publicly funded program, these are very small potatoes indeed.

Despite these facts, government and the health insurance system insist on making us cost-conscious. As with everything else, the retired, the disabled, and those with low incomes are hurt most by cost-consciousness. They wait the longest before they seek help and they do without help most often simply because they are the most "cost-conscious" of all. What it will cost is ever before them when they consider their need for help.

When Americans who can pay little or nothing for care are struck by illness or accident, they have two choices. They can seek treatment from private hospitals and physicians at the risk of being turned away because they cannot pay or they can seek free care from a city or charity hospital where care is frequently demeaning and inadequate. Unfortunately, many Americans avoid both alternatives. Rather than risk humiliation, they simply avoid taking members of their family for care at all, except in grave emergencies when they have no choice.

The hard fact is that hospitals and doctors have bills to pay and salaries to earn, too. If they can't collect, they can't keep their doors open for long. That is why they carefully check a patient's insurance coverages. Sometimes, if he looks as though he can't pay, they check before they will treat him. That is why many hospitals hire collection agencies or sell their "bad debts" to collection agencies for only a portion of their value. They can use every penny they can get. That is also why some hospitals and some physicians avoid those who can't pay, discourage them from coming, rush their treatment, or, if necessary, actually turn them away.

Most Americans do not think of health care as a business— as something you buy the way you buy the services of a law-yer or a carpenter. Unfortunately, for many hospitals facing budget crises, and for many physicians, it *is* a business. They have a service to sell to those who come to them ready to pay. Like any business, many feel no obligation to serve those who cannot pay. We heard of a surgeon who wouldn't go upstairs to operate until he had his $800 fee, doctors who require the poor to give the receptionist his fee before they will even see them, a dentist who ordered an elderly Medicaid patient out of his chair, hospitals that require fifty- and seventy-five-dollar deposits before they'll accept an emergency case, and professional collection agencies that hound patients to step up payments on hospital bills. Most Americans never experience this "business" attitude in this extreme way because most have some insurance coverage and some ability to pay. However, an American can experience it if he happens to lose his job or his insurance, if he is disabled and forced to retire early on limited income, or if he is bankrupted by costs of illness or other tragedy. Millions of Americans who simply have low-paying jobs live with this reality every day.

The emergency room or outpatient clinic of the public hospitals become the last resort for people who can't get help elsewhere. In some cities, such facilities are clean, modern, and centers of high-quality care. In many cities they are run-down, dirty, understaffed and half-forgotten by the city that runs them. In almost every case they involve long waits, and they offer a form of care which most physicians would consider unacceptable as the primary source of health care for a family.

I would like to share a few of the cases I have seen and heard.

### AMERICANS WHO ARE TURNED AWAY BECAUSE THEY CANNOT PAY

Sometimes the hospital is not sure a family can pay or not. If the family is black or looks poor, the hospital might choose to be certain before offering treatment. In the following case of Mr. Paul Johnson of Chicago, this type of delay possibly contributed to a ten-year-old boy's death.

SENATOR KENNEDY: Tell us about what happened to your son.

MR. JOHNSON: On December 15, 1969, he had a seizure at home and he passed out. I picked him up, rushed him to the nearest hospital. I went by a police station and was led to a hospital by the name of St. George's here in the neighborhood. I asked the police to carry me out to County Hospital and he said he couldn't go out of his district.

The doctor didn't even look at him or put his hand on him at St. George's, but in the meantime I was in and they interviewed me to find out my history of my financial arrangements, my insurance and this and that. I had Traveler's Insurance at the time. . . .

So we left this hospital and drove all the way from seventy-ninth over here to County Hospital, where my son died in a matter of an hour or so afterwards. . . .

SENATOR KENNEDY: You went to the emergency room of St. George's Hospital and you asked for service?

MR. JOHNSON: Yes.

SENATOR KENNEDY: That is, you asked for someone to take a look at your boy, is that right?

MR. JOHNSON: Yes, but they interviewed me beforehand.

SENATOR KENNEDY: When you did this, in effect your son was actually in the process of dying and they were asking you questions about where you lived?

MR. JOHNSON: Yes.

SENATOR KENNEDY: And about the kind of insurance you had?

MR. JOHNSON: Yes, sir—"Do you own your own home?" and this and that, and "Who do you work for?" and "How long?" . . . I asked them, if they needed further information and what not they could call out to County Hospital, that he had been a patient there and he was due to go in for a check-up which was that Friday, the nineteenth, and he didn't make it. They would have given them the information if they needed it, but they didn't even try to do anything. County Hospital had voluntarily told me also that if anything happens to Carl, even to have a tooth extracted or a tooth filled or anything, to call them and they would give the doctors the information that is necessary so it wouldn't be fatal to him.

SENATOR KENNEDY: Then you took your son over to the other hospital, to County Hospital, is that right?

MR. JOHNSON: Yes.

SENATOR KENNEDY: Going by several other hospitals?

MR. JOHNSON: Yes, because I was afraid to stop. I think the same thing would have happened if I had stopped at one of the other hospitals. . . . I might as well try to make it to the County.

I drove down the expressway with my oldest son. . . . I had my oldest son with me, and my younger son was in pain and he was going into a coma, and he was hysterical and everything, and the older boy was holding him. . . .

SENATOR KENNEDY: As he was hysterical, the doctor at St. George's said, "If you don't like the service here, take him elsewhere"?

MR. JOHNSON: Yes. He told me that "he couldn't be sick with a heart condition if he is able to scream and holler like that." That is what he said.

SENATOR KENNEDY: So then you went to Cook County Hospital?

MR. JOHNSON: Cook County Hospital, and they decided right away to put a pacemaker in and whatnot, but he went into a coma and passed away before they got a chance to insert it.

SENATOR KENNEDY: Now, did you ever hear from St. George's again?

MR. JOHNSON: Yes, I heard from them. I paid the emergency-room bill. . . .

SENATOR KENNEDY: They sent you a bill after this? . . .

MR. JOHNSON: Yes, one was a doctor's bill and one was the emergency-room bill.

SENATOR KENNEDY: How much were they?

MR. JOHNSON: Twelve-fifty for the emergency room and seven dollars for the doctor's fee. . . .

SENATOR KENNEDY: Do you think a hospital ought to be able to pick and choose its patients?

MR. JOHNSON: No, I don't. I think a hospital is in the neighborhood and I think it is supposed to serve the people that are living in the neighborhood, who are supporting it. . . .

SENATOR KENNEDY: Do you think there is something wrong with a health system in our country or at St. George's or anywhere that says, "You have got to pay before you are going to get treated"?

MR. JOHNSON: Yes, I think so, because if I don't have the money and I am sick, I think I need the medical care. Give me a chance to pay it later if I am unable to provide it now.

Mrs. Dolores Kemphfer, in West Virginia, told how lack of money kept her from getting care for herself and her five children while her husband was employed with a railroad. She related the following incidents.

MRS. KEMPHFER: I have had five children in eight years. I came from a very poor family. I have this one child, Cindy Robbins, she was my second. She has bronchial asthma. I had just had my fourth baby. Cindy took pneumonia. I was staying with my husband's brother and his wife, Irma, at the time. They took Cindy to the hospital. Irma comes back and says. "Dolores, we have got to have fifty dollars before Cindy can have oxygen." . . .

My husband had just went back to work. I had to locate him. He was working in Marlinton. I had to get the money from his boss. By that time, I went on to the hospital and made my phone calls. I was holding my little girl and I started crying. The doctor said, "If you can't take care of them, why did you have them damned kids?" Those were the words. He was very disgusted with me. I am there without money and with a sick child. . . .

I have been kept out of the hospitals because I have no insurance, no money from the bank, to get them in.

SENATOR KENNEDY: You can't get them into the hospital?

MRS. KEMPHFER: It is awful hard to get them in.

SENATOR KENNEDY: Do they ask you, when you come down to get them into the hospital—

MRS. KEMPHFER: If you have insurance or the money.

SENATOR KENNEDY: They ask you that before they treat the child.

MRS. KEMPHFER: We have to have seventy-five dollars at one hospital and fifty dollars at another.

SENATOR KENNEDY: In the emergency room?

MRS. KEMPHFER: Usually, when I go to the emergency room, yes.

SENATOR KENNEDY: Before you are able to get them in at one hospital you have to pay fifty dollars and the other is seventy-five dollars.

MRS. KEMPHFER: That is right. After Peggy Sue, this is my fifth one, I went to this old doctor and he was real nice. My husband had started to work for a mining company which had insurance. It was a bad-risk insurance coverage, because of the asthmatic and because I needed an operation. So we was a bad risk. We would have to have the policy two or three years before it would do us any good.

. . . I was supposed to have a tubal ligation after Peggy Sue was born, and the doctor that I was going to didn't perform this kind of an operation, but he informed another doctor that I needed it. He said he would accept my insurance policy. We didn't have cash at the time. So my doctor says, "Dolores, you need it, I will pay for your operation and I will wait for the insurance to come through." You know, I had Peggy Sue that night. The next morning my doctor died of a heart attack. The other doctor came in and they gave me a hypo in the arm, and I thought they were getting ready for the operation. Fifteen minutes later he said, "Your source of money is gone, it just died. You either come up with the money or get out of the hospital." I picked my baby up the next day and left the hospital."

SENATOR KENNEDY: Is the only time you go to the hospital or to the doctor when you have an emergency situation?

MRS. KEMPHFER: I have to limit it to that.

SENATOR KENNEDY: Have your children ever seen a dentist?

MRS. KEMPHFER: No, not really. I just got my teeth last summer. All mine went with the babies. My husband is also sickly. He gets pneumonia awful easy.

SENATOR KENNEDY: What does he do?

MRS. KEMPHFER: He won't go to the doctor. He gets delirious and I drag him to the doctor and he doesn't know where he is.

SENATOR KENNEDY: Why doesn't he go to the doctor?

MRS. KEMPHFER: He is scared.

SENATOR KENNEDY: Is it part of the fact he will have medical bills, too?

MRS. KEMPHFER: Yes. He told me one time when I was pregnant, and he said, "I don't like children." I said, "Why?" He says, "Ours have always been sickly, we watch them almost die with no money." It just tears us apart, you know, to have them.

SENATOR RANDOLPH: Your children are in school and have shots given to them?

MRS. KEMPHFER: Yes, I do get that. Little Peggy Sue is allergic to the shots. I have to watch her awful carefully, you know. I sponge her down or she will go into convulsions.

SENATOR RANDOLPH: What recommendation do you have for us for an improvement in, let's say, health or hospitalization that will help people like you that face these problems?

MRS. KEMPHFER: I am all for this preventive medicine they have out now. After Amanda had the rheumatic fever I went to the doctor, and I tried to take the pill many a time and I couldn't. They worked on my nerves. This last time I broke out in a rash and swelled up. I took them four months before I would give in and realize I couldn't take them.

So I said, "I can't see having another child like this. And I can't take the pill." So he said, "Well, it's up to you, you'll have to get the IUD, it's going to cost you from forty to fifty dollars. Can you come up with it?" I said yes.

I went back home and I picked up the newspaper and read where they are having a family-planning clinic on June 26. I called my doctor and asked if I could go there. He said yes. I was the first one there. I wanted to make sure they didn't run out of these things.

SENATOR KENNEDY: Do they usually run out?

MRS. KEMPHFER: I don't know. But in my case, I was going to make sure they didn't. I didn't run out of babies. [Laughter.]

SENATOR RANDOLPH: You wanted to be there when the door opened?

MRS. KEMPHFER: Yes. I was there when the door opened. It wouldn't work. So I went home all upset. So I go back to the doctor. He says, "There is nothing you can do." We didn't have any insurance.

So about a week or two later infection set in. I went back and he wouldn't even see me. I went on for another week until I couldn't move. I was so sore inside I couldn't move. So I went down and waited until his office opened up the next morning. He examined me and said, "You have got acute infection. It is set in clear in your whole system. You are going to have to have an operation. You take this penicillin and call me Tuesday at ten o'clock and I will have you admitted."

I called Tuesday at ten o'clock. He said, "You have no insurance, no money, they won't accept you."

So I said, "Would you get in contact with the family-planning clinic in Morgantown? They will contact a doctor for me." So he did. I went to Morgantown. That was August 19. They listened to all of my problems, all of my children, why I didn't want any more, and I was sent up to have a tubal ligation and a D and C, and in my condition I had to have a partial hysterectomy. . . .

SENATOR KENNEDY: Your husband, as I understand it, was working one time and then they garnisheed the money from his salary. Was that to pay off medical bills?

MRS. KEMPHFER: He was fired from his job because we owed a hospital bill on one of our children. They attached his wages. The policy is you straighten it up yourself with the people or they don't need your employment anymore. I tried to straighten it up. It had already gone through the court. It had to come off his wages.

SENATOR KENNEDY: He was fired?

MRS. KEMPHFER: Yes. That is where we got our insurance, too. . . .

SENATOR KENNEDY: Just because you were unable to pay, he lost his job.

Rural Americans are not alone in being treated this way because they cannot pay. It happens also in the suburbs and the inner city. In Hempstead, New York, a social worker observed that some old people are so devastated at being turned away by doctors that they never go back. She brought several elderly ladies with her who were afraid to give their names in front of the health professionals present. One, whom we called "Mrs. Jones," told the following story of trying to get dental care.

MRS. JONES: Well, I have been a widow now since I was fifty-one years old. And I had to go to work, and I did, and I worked for about eighteen years. And a widow without anything, no insurance to speak of, or anything, left me totally dependent on my little income from work. And paying my doctor bills and everything else took all of it during the years, all of it. I did manage to get along until about four or five years ago, but since then I have absolutely nothing, and I am very concerned about Medicaid because this is the only secure thing that I have to keep my health and well-being, and I have had trouble with getting my dental work done. I have gone from one to another.

SENATOR KENNEDY: What sort of trouble have you had?

MRS. JONES: Well, I have been going to the same dentist that I had been going to when I paid my own bills years ago, and he told me that I couldn't have it anymore . . . when I got on Medicaid. And I got the same story from another one. And the last one I called he told me to come down—the young lady told me to come. And I did go, and I walked up the stairs. When I got up there he had me in the chair and was speaking about Medicaid. He immediately said, "I can't touch you, I won't touch you, you will have to go." And, of course, I felt—well, you can imagine how I felt. And I have been embarrassed many times with medication and things like that in spite of Medicaid.

These cases are not rare. An employee of the New York City Health and Hospitals Corporation who handles complaints against proprietary hospitals in New York City described similar cases. The director of the Emergency Food Program in one county in West Virginia described a hospital which requires prior financial arrangements of everyone receiving services. Field workers in the food program have rushed one man suffering a stroke and one woman delivering a baby to other hospitals when they were turned away for the lack of a $50 deposit.

Finally, let me offer one last case.

Mr. James Parsons, a bridge painter in Nashville, described his experience with his wife's pregnancies, and how she was evicted from hospitals because she could not pay.

SENATOR KENNEDY: You're Mr. James Parsons and you work for the bridge company?

MR. PARSONS: Nashville Bridge Company.

SENATOR KENNEDY: Could you tell us a little bit about some of your problems?

MR. PARSONS: Well, it started in 1964 when my wife went to the hospital for childbirth. The hospital bill was about six hundred dollars and the doctor bill was two hundred fifty. Three months later she went back to the hospital for an operation for tubal pregnancy. She came out of the hospital three days before she was supposed to because we didn't have money to pay the hospital bills, because we didn't have insurance. The doctor told her he'd have to take her out of the hospital.

SENATOR KENNEDY: What happened to your insurance?

MR. PARSONS: I was working at Wedgewood Corporation at the time and they went out of business. I had insurance with Wedgewood Corporation and they went out of business, and they told us our policy was good for ninety days after the company went out of business. So I was out of work a month and a half and that's when my wife went to the hospital, and then we found out we didn't have any insurance.

SENATOR KENNEDY: How long did you work for that company?

MR. PARSONS: Three years.

SENATOR KENNEDY: Then they went out of business and your wife had this additional difficulty or complication, and do I understand that she went to the hospital and the doctor or someone in the hospital said she'd have to leave?

MR. PARSONS: Yes, the doctor . . .

SENATOR KENNEDY: This is after your wife had been admitted, she had some complications and the doctor told you you'd have to take her out of the hospital. What did you do?

MR. PARSONS: Well, they checked her out of the hospital.

SENATOR KENNEDY: You mean you took her out of the hospital?

MR. PARSONS: Yes, sir, because we didn't have any money to keep her in any longer. So we took her home and then she had a setback.

SENATOR KENNEDY: What do you mean, a setback?

MR. PARSONS: She started hemorrhaging, and the doctor wouldn't put her back in the hospital, he treated her at home.

SENATOR KENNEDY: Why wouldn't he put her back in the hospital?

MR. PARSONS: Because we couldn't pay the hospital bill. . . . And then seven months later she went back to the hospital for another operation for a tubal pregnancy and she couldn't stay in the full length of time. They had to send her home again because we didn't have insurance. . . .

SENATOR KENNEDY: Tell us what happened this time.

MR. PARSONS: Well the doctors put her in the hospital, they didn't know what was wrong with her the second time. She had been to his office that Friday morning and she went back home and started being faint, so she called me at work and told me about it.

SENATOR KENNEDY: You were working now?

MR. PARSONS: Yes, sir. So I told her to get the girl across the hall to stay with her until I could come home. In the meantime she got so bad the girl across the hall called the doctor and he said for her to elevate her feet, and then the girl called the ambulance so she could go to the hospital, and she went to the hospital and stayed in there, it was four days, and then they dismissed her because we didn't have the money. . . .

SENATOR KENNEDY: You had some rather extraordinary medical bills?

MR. PARSONS: Yes, sir, I had about $3,200 worth of medical bills.

SENATOR KENNEDY: Not covered by insurance?

MR. PARSONS: Not covered by insurance. That was hospital bills and doctor bills and drugs, and they pressured me so bad.

SENATOR KENNEDY: Who is "they"?

MR. PARSONS: The doctors and hospitals and collection agencies pressured me so bad.

SENATOR KENNEDY: What do you mean by "pressure"?

MR. PARSONS: Well, I was paying twenty dollars a month and I was making seventy dollars a week.

SENATOR KENNEDY: You were making seventy dollars a week?

MR. PARSONS: Yes, sir, and I dropped down. I was not paying anything, because I couldn't afford it, and then they turned it over to the collectors, and they garnisheed my wages. They threatened us on the telephone, sent us letters.

SENATOR KENNEDY: What sort of things would they say when they called up and threatened?

MR. PARSONS: That the bill was past due, and they wanted payment in full.

SENATOR KENNEDY: You were trying to pay at least something whenever you could, is that right?

MR. PARSONS: Yes, whenever I could. At the time they were calling on the telephone I couldn't pay anything at all, and that's when they started pressuring.

SENATOR KENNEDY: So what finally happened?

MR. PARSONS: I had to take bankruptcy in order to get out from under the pressure of the doctors and the collectors. . . .

SENATOR KENNEDY: So where are you now, Mr. Parsons —what kind of shape are you in now?

MR. PARSONS: I'm in fairly good shape now. That was in 1967 when I had taken bankruptcy.

SENATOR KENNEDY: How many years have you been a workingman?

MR. PARSONS: I have been working since I was fifteen years old. . . .

SENATOR KENNEDY: Do you have children now?

MR. PARSONS: A little girl six, and she goes to the doctor now, probably once a month, and they won't let her in to see the doctor unless we have money to pay them in advance.

SENATOR KENNEDY: Who won't let them in to see the doctor?

MR. PARSONS: Miller's Clinic. It costs eleven dollars for her to get in to see the doctor, and you have to sit out there about three hours and he's with her about five minutes.

SENATOR KENNEDY: That's about a hundred dollars an hour for the doctor. That's no matter how sick the child is?

MR. PARSONS: No matter how sick.

SENATOR KENNEDY: You have to get up the eleven dollars.

MR. PARSONS: Yes, sir.

SENATOR KENNEDY: There couldn't be a question in anybody's mind that this is not how the richest society in the world ought to be caring for the health of the people. Some people say the fact that you have to pay the eleven dollars for your child to go down and see a doctor is cost-consciousness. They say that's going to make you a lot more cost-conscious. They think someone like yourself who has been working all your life ought to have to pay that because they think you'll overutilize the facility. They think you want to give up your hours of work and get your wife down sitting in a doctor's office because it's fun. I don't understand that particular argument.

MR. PARSONS: It's rather embarrassing. She goes out there and sits out there almost an hour and then they'll call her up to the desk and remind her that she has to have the money before she can get in. . . .

These are extreme cases—where the hospital, physician or dentist actually turns away a patient in need of care. There are other, subtler ways of avoiding giving care to those who cannot pay, however. Many physicians and hospitals simply move out of low-income areas and into wealthier communities. Many hospitals simply close their emergency rooms or outpatient clinics and accept patients only when referred by a private physician. Their actions reduce the number of people whom the physician or hospital sees who cannot pay. If we think of health care as a business, such moves make good sense. If you have a service to sell, you go to people who can afford to buy it—you can't afford to just give it away.

So many physicians and hospitals have resorted to this type of action, however, that in many cities the public or city hospital is almost the only source of health care for millions of Americans.

THOSE WHO RESORT TO A PUBLIC HOSPITAL

If you cannot pay, you may be able to get to a public hospital that will treat the poor—or to an enlightened private hospital. In some cities, voluntary hospitals do attempt to serve the poor and write off charges that they cannot collect.

All hospitals which serve those who cannot pay, however, whether public or private, share similar problems. They have great difficulty balancing their budgets. When the subcommittee was in Cleveland, the private university hospitals had just announced that a fifty percent reduction in outpatient services would be necessary unless they found some financial relief.

Many private hospitals ultimately are forced to pass to the public hospitals the burden of treating those who cannot pay. Dr. Nick Rango, of the Interns' Association of Cook County Hospitals, in Chicago, said, "It is not unusual for those of us at County Hospital to have patients dumped on us from private hospitals with a little note saying, 'His insurance benefits have run out, but he is a good patient, and please do the best you can.'" These kinds of things happen every day.

The public hospital is the last stop, however, and they have no way of escaping the hard financial realities of offering expensive services to those who cannot pay for them. We have heard the directors of such hospitals describe their serious financial problems—so serious as to threaten the hospitals' very existence. While some public hospitals across the nation remain excellent institutions, many such hospitals in our cities are reaching the point of disaster, with staffs rebelling and in some cases bringing lawsuits against the facility for failing to provide adequate services.

This situation has led to two systems of hospital care in America. We have seen well-equipped private hospitals, fully staffed and with little or no waiting lines, just blocks away from facilities crumbling for the lack of funds, understaffed, and with waiting periods of six to eight hours or longer. In one city we visited, there were two facilities; one boasted beautiful new construction and collected ninety-five percent of all their charges, the other was old and run-down and was operated by the city for the poor only.

THE INDIGNITIES OF CHARITY CARE

In the midst of the long lines, shortage of staff, and lack of facilities and equipment, treatment in some public and voluntary hospitals can become impersonal, hasty, and sometimes demeaning.

Mr. Samuel F. Bordy stood up at our hearing in West Virginia to say the following.

MR. BORDY: There is a certain hospital, I am not mentioning any names. I had two heart attacks, and after the second one I had I went to the emergency room. They wouldn't even let me in the emergency room, because I was on welfare. It took me an hour and a half before I could get hold of a nurse. Then she treated me like I was a dog or something—take you out in the hallway and strip down and give you a shot in the hallway, and turn you loose like you was a wild animal or something.

So I don't think that is right.

Mrs. Alexander Petrich of San Francisco also described treatment in one such hospital.

MRS. PETRICH: Three and a half years ago, when I was pregnant, we didn't have any kind of insurance. We weren't eligible to go to Kaiser or anyplace like that and couldn't afford the bill for the payment to a private doctor.

So I went to the outpatient clinic at St. Mary's Hospital, which is a very large clinic and has a very large turnover of patients. It is staffed and run, from what I have been able to tell, by interns, and it is designed to serve as a learning place for interns. . . .

The women . . . would all be given an appointment at nine o'clock in the morning and if you were lucky and happened to get there early you might be able to see a doctor by ten-thirty—or sometimes you had to wait until eleven-thirty or so.

After this you see the doctor for five minutes. I never saw the same doctor twice. I think maybe once I saw the same person twice, but it was always a different person and there was never any kind of an attempt made to treat anybody who is there like they were a person or like they deserved any kind of attention as being a person—it was just being a pregnant "being" who had to get this baby delivered.

One time, toward the end of my pregnancy, one of the interns or doctors examining me decided there was something slightly irregular about the position of the baby; and so he went out, without saying anything to me, and called in five or six other people, who all proceeded to poke and stick their fingers in me. I was only nineteen years old, and it was my first pregnancy. I sort of resented the fact of a roomful of strange men just coming in and doing this.

Another thing was that at no time was an effort made to explain to me the process of what was happening; and I always was reluctant to ask any questions, because the attitude was sort of to get you in and get you out and don't bother us with your questions.

This made it hard. When women are pregnant they get kind of insecure and nervous, and I was not experienced and I just felt very uneasy about the whole thing. . . .

SENATOR KENNEDY: Did you talk with the other women down there, too? Did they share this feeling of impersonalization?

MRS. PETRICH: They seemed kind of—a lot of them, you could tell, were very poor and a lot of them had so many children, and they seemed afraid and kind of reluctant to impose themselves on this big, you know, impersonal kind of system that obviously knew so much more than they did.

SENATOR KENNEDY: Why do you think people are afraid?

MRS. PETRICH: I just got the feeling [that the reason] I wasn't being told [was that] because I was poor I was dumb; therefore I shouldn't bother anybody. And I am not dumb. But that was the kind of impression that I was given. . . .

SENATOR KENNEDY: Your husband works for the post office.

MRS. PETRICH: Yes. He was making about $2.65 an hour, which isn't enough. I didn't want to get a doctor bill of a thousand dollars—which it would cost, close to that, for a private doctor.

SENATOR KENNEDY: Wouldn't he be covered by some program?

MRS. PETRICH: I can't remember why—he wasn't covered, for some reason. There was some kind of reason, there was some problem and he wasn't covered, but I am really not sure why. . . . I went to the outpatient clinic. It was considered a very good one. It was referred to me by several people—and it just turned out to be a bad experience.

### THE INADEQUACIES OF CHARITY CARE

More important than the indignities patients may suffer when they cannot pay, however, most public hospitals cannot offer comprehensive care. They do not often encourage mothers to bring in their children for regular checkups, shots, and other preventive care, for example. They seldom have time and staff to schedule such visits. Nor do they have time to talk to a distraught mother on the telephone about her child's illness and advise her whether he should be brought in for examination—a service which many mothers who can pay enjoy and use frequently with their pediatrician.

Because this kind of health care is all that is available to those who cannot pay, it is certain that there are many Americans who don't even try to get health care except in emergencies.

Dr. Sanford Kravitz in Hempstead, Long Island, dramatized for us the difference it makes if you can pay for your children's health care. Every parent is all too familiar with the earaches, sore throats, coughs, minor injuries, or mild temperatures that seem to be regular occurrences among the children. In Hempstead, a suburb of New York City, the mother who can pay has a pediatrician. Dr. Kravitz suggests that ninety percent of child health care begins when the mother calls the doctor, describes the problem, and asks, "Should I bring the child in?" The doctor makes the judgment, often suggesting some home remedy with a caution to watch for rising fever or other symptoms which indicate that the child should be examined. This kind of advice for many Americans is only a phone call away, and it is offered by the same office that schedules regular child examinations, shots, corrective shoes, braces, and whatever else is necessary to allow the child to grow to a healthy adult.

Consider by comparison the plight of the low-income mother confronting the same situation with her children. She most likely has no pediatrician to call—nor any other private physician. She can call the outpatient clinic at the hospital but won't be able to speak to a doctor and will end up taking the child in. If she has other children, that means taking them along or getting a baby-sitter, which she cannot afford. To get there will likely be a long ride in the bus with the sick child—she cannot afford the taxi. And when she arrives it will mean a long, long wait with the child in a crowded waiting room—all perhaps to find out that the child has a virus for which aspirin and bed rest are all that's needed. In the face of these problems, according to Dr. Kravitz, many mothers simply don't go until there is an obvious emergency.

There are, of course, many others who bypass care rather than go to the city hospital: the elderly who are too feeble for the long bus ride and the long wait, the worker who cannot take off a whole day to wait in long lines, those who don't have and cannot afford transportation, the proud who are stung by the impersonality and the indignities they've suffered before.

The extent of this problem is evidenced in studies done by the Meharry Medical College in Nashville. Dr. Lloyd C. Elam testified that out of 65,000 low-income people in the immediate community, one quarter of the children had no baby shots and one third of all the people had never had chest X rays, tetanus shots, or polio vaccine. Moreover, sixty-one percent of the people between ages twenty-five and forty-five reported current health problems for which they are not seeking help. Dr. Elam attributed these neglects primarily to the cost of care.

We heard from a woman in Cleveland whose small business was lost as a result of a serious case of diabetes that took both her legs. She wanted to return to work, but her insurance would not cover the $1,200 she needed for artificial legs. No American should be kept from participating fully in our society by such a thing.

The fact is, the general health care currently offered in many of the outpatient departments or emergency rooms for those who cannot pay is so inadequate that many simply do not get health care at all.

## MY CONVICTION

*Americans should not be kept from getting adequate health care because of its cost. Our society should assure every American good health care at a cost which does not discourage him from seeking care.*

*It is unconscionable that in our rich nation a rich man's child has a better chance for a full and healthy life than a child whose family must worry about bills and delay or do without health care because they fear the expense. Whether or not a child's leg is straightened, for example, should not depend on whether his father feels he can afford the bill. Cost-consciousness should not be a reason for limiting a child's chance for good health.*

*Moreover, in a country as rich as America, and with a vision of equal opportunity such as America has, we cannot watch the cost of health care keep Americans bound to a life of poverty by keeping them from education and fruitful work.*

*Americans who are disabled, Americans who are elderly, Americans who have met financial disaster, and Americans who are unemployed and as a result uninsured—none of these deserves to bear the burden of bad health or to watch their loved ones grow up in bad health or with needlessly twisted limbs. They have done nothing to deserve this suffering or the indignities of a second-class health system created just for them.*

*Nor does the answer lie in two systems of care, one for those who can pay and one for those who cannot. Two systems of care will inevitably turn into two levels of care. If it is good to provide health care to all Americans, it is also good to provide it without the indignities and hardships of a two-class system.*

*If a man does not have his health he cannot hold a job or give his all to his work, and consequently he cannot buy housing, food, or education for himself and his children. When low-income families are asked what they need most, health care is invariably near the top of their lists of needs. I believe America is rich enough and wise enough to offer this to them at a cost they can afford as part of the equal opportunity we cherish for all Americans.*

*Others hesitate to respond to the needs of low-income Americans for fear they may overutilize health services because they don't appreciate the costs. Millions of Americans, however, are painfully conscious of costs today—so much so they simply don't get care at all. For them, the deductibles, coinsurance, and part payments of health insurance don't make them more cost-conscious, they simply keep them away from care altogether. We must lay to rest once and for all the myth that we must keep people away lest they abuse the system. It simply isn't true. I believe America can afford to offer care to these Americans at a cost they can afford, lest we exclude them from our society altogether. I am convinced that cost should not be a consideration when any American, regardless of income, considers whether or not to seek care.*

CHAPTER IV

# Where Have All

# the Doctors Gone?

THE burden is on Americans to seek out and find help when they are sick. Help seldom, if ever, seeks them out. If you live in one of the 130 rural counties that have no doctors, you may have to drive a long way to find help. If you live in the inner city, you may find that the doctors are all gone, and that help can be had only by going to the city hospital and waiting for hours. If you are sick while out of town or after hours, you will have trouble getting a doctor to see you. If you are very elderly, disabled, or very ill and ask a physician to come to you, you will most likely get no taker. You will have to get an ambulance and get to the hospital on your own. Nor does health care necessarily come to you in the ambulance. In many cities the ambulances are staffed by people who know little or nothing about health care. The ambulance is simply a tool for you to use to seek out health care.

In all of these situations, physicians and hospitals demonstrate the belief that their obligation begins when someone comes to them for help. Their obligation apparently does not include seeking out the sick to make sure they get the care they need, nor does it include even making it easy to reach help when illness strikes at inconvenient times and places.

As a result, those who cannot pound at the door of the system because they are elderly or disabled, or without money, or ignorant of their needs, or simply neglectful of themselves or their families, will not get health care. Those who pound and pound but live in the wrong place or get sick at the wrong time may not get care, either.

Not all providers of care refuse to seek out the health needs among the people. There are many professionals working in this way. We have frequently been told by medical societies that everyone who looks for help gets it in their area—only to have socially concerned physicians, dentists, and nurses show us the unmet needs and the neglected and abused people they work with every day. The difference is that organized medicine counts only those who fight their way through all obstacles to get to the physician's door with money in their hand, while many individual doctors, dentists, and nurses count all Americans regardless of their income, where they live, or their ability to overcome all obstacles to get to a doctor.

I have been especially impressed with the public-health nurses across our nation, who frequently go where no one else will go, and who spend hours working to obtain more health care for their patients. These good people have led me by the arm into homes and entire communities that seldom or never see a physician or dentist, and whose twisted limbs and bad health are painfully apparent to the nurse, to the occasional doctor who goes along, and even to my untrained eye.

The professionals who seek out the people with health care needs in their community rather than insisting that the people come to them are always the first to insist that the health care system must be changed so that more health care is offered to Americans.

I suspect that every American family can recount tales of frustration and terror trying to reach doctors, even when they are nearby and available. Let me share a few of the situations I heard that led me to my belief that health services must come to the patient.

### SEEKING OUT HEALTH CARE AFTER HOURS

Even if there is a physician near you, you may have trouble getting to him if you are sick at inconvenient times. At our hearing in Iowa, the state medical society indicated that no one in Iowa was more than twenty minutes from a doctor. In response, my distinguished colleague Senator Harold E. Hughes told the following story.

SENATOR HUGHES: Would it surprise you if I were to tell you that when I was governor of this state I tried to call a physician for my son-in-law in this city and could not get a physician to go to his home to see him when he was suffering some severe cramps and intestinal distress? We were afraid to move him, and I called the Polk County Medical Society for help. There was no physician that they would give me for help; I was told as governor of this state to go to the house and get him and bring him to the emergency entrance of this very hospital. No one would see him. . . . When that happens to the governor, you know, I wonder what happens to the rest of the people.

So much of the medical care in this state is excellent and

magnificent in quality, and yet we have so many that are totally left out. That's what we are talking about.

I might add, just to make the record equal, that last year in the state of Virginia my second daughter was seized one night with severe pain in the abdomen. We called an ambulance. We rushed her to a hospital, where we could get no medical help because we couldn't find a doctor who knew us. The doctor whom we called on—and, as a United States Senator, I called the Senate physician—couldn't make a recommendation to me. The pain was almost impossible to bear, yet they would give her absolutely nothing to relieve the pain. Seven hours later I was calling physicians in Des Moines, Iowa, trying to find out the types of pain relievers and drugs given to her during earlier illnesses. I finally tracked down at Okoboji the physician who had treated her in Iowa, after at least fifteen long-distance calls. I called Dr. Bedell at the University Hospitals for help. He had been my own physician for many years. When finally medical care was found and a diagnosis was made, she had suffered from an inversion of the small intestine, and gangrene set in three days later.

I threatened a doctor in the hallway of that hospital and told him I'd break his neck if he didn't come in and do something about my daughter. I'm pretty upset when I find conditions like this in America.

Indeed, if a governor or a United States Senator cannot get a doctor after regular office hours, what of the average citizens?

In California, Mr. Gerardo Martinez told of his efforts to get by a doctor's receptionist during lunch hour because of an emergency with his child.

MR. MARTINEZ: My name is Gerardo Martinez, and I live in the San Fernando Valley. . . . The particular experience which I have—negative experience, if I may say—in regards to medical health is that my daughter, which was born out of six months' pregnancy, weighed one pound and four ounces, which was given only one chance out of twenty to live. She is an adopted daughter. . . .

We are fortunate enough, my family, of being one of a very few within the Mexican-American community that do have job-related insurance. We are insured with a group carrier, Kaiser. I had to take my daughter in at the age of eight months, who is still very much underweight, . . . because she developed clear signs of being very ill: high temperature, very high, 103, difficulty in breathing, every sign for a lay person to notice that the child was very sick.

I have to call first. I call first to find out if they will be able to get the charts, or whatever, and be ready when we arrived. I was informed that I could not take the child, as it was noon and the doctors had to take a lunch break and they were only able to take care of emergencies. This is a lay person that answers the phones and this type of service, and he is not a registered nurse or anybody else that have any type of medical treatment—as I was able to find out later—or medical education that would be able to diagnose, even by phone, which I am sure even the best doctor will not attempt, to be able to judge that a child in that particular case as I explained it would be able to wait an hour and a half until the doctor will see her.

I decided not to wait for him to call the doctor for him to tell me his advice whether to take her or not, but to take her immediately. There again I have to face just the receptionist, no one that has been trained in any way in the medical field. I was asked again if I had called and if the doctor had advised me to bring the child in. I refer again to the previous conversation a few minutes earlier over the phone, and the people got very upset. Nevertheless, I was able to force my way, and I do mean force my way, in order to get a doctor to see the child. The baby was found to have what the doctor, after he knew everything that had been going on between me and the receptionist, qualified as a touch of pneumonia, was put under oxygen and was kept in the hospital.

Now, I don't know, doctors on the outside which I have talked to about it assured me that under those circumstances it could have been fatal. This I do not know. But I do know that the child was very sick and needed treatment and yet the treatment that you are getting through your insurance, which is not free because we are paying thirty-five dollars a month for this, plus seven dollars that the employer pays for it, we are not able to get it.

SENATOR KENNEDY: You could tell when your child was sick, couldn't you?

MR. MARTINEZ: Yes. . . .

SENATOR KENNEDY: And all you were trying to do was to get some treatment for her?

MR. MARTINEZ: Yes. But the point, Senator, is that many of our people in the Mexican community cannot bypass those barriers that are being put in front of us like the one that was put in front of me. I happen to be pushy, and I can find my way through. But they will not find their way through in more than sixty percent of the cases, and that child could have died if it would be somebody else's child.

Most Americans can add stories of their own to these—stories about discussions or arguments with answering services or receptionists over whether you can speak to the doctor or whether you should come to the office. Frequently it is left to us and the physician's receptionist to decide whether it is urgent enough to disturb the doctor; of course, neither we nor the receptionist is really qualified to make that decision. How many Americans have hung up the phone and waited until morning worrying and in pain, or watching their children in pain, after the answering service talked them out of speaking with the doctor. No doubt many of us in such situations have cursed ourselves for not being as determined and forceful as Mr. Martinez. Many who live in Suburbia resort to their local hospital in such after-hour situations and find the long waiting lines which are the regular experience of their less fortunate neighbors in the inner city.

Again, even when physicians and hospitals are at hand, it frequently seems that, rather than their seeking out the people and making it as easy as possible for people to reach them, people must fight through obstacles to get to them. The receptionist, the answering service, the unlisted home number, the refusal of service to a new patient from out of town without a referral—all seem better suited to protecting the providers' peace and quiet than to seeking out those who need care. They in fact become obstacles to be overcome when we seek health care.

SEEKING OUT HEALTH CARE WHEN YOU'RE
ELDERLY OR DISABLED

Perhaps the biggest obstacles to care are faced by the disabled and the elderly in our cities. Their age leaves them at a disadvantage to start with. To find a doctor in the city, the disabled and elderly are frequently forced to the city hospital. Mr. Charles Gildersleeve of the Fulton Senior Center in New

York City said he knows elderly citizens who waited all day at a public hospital and went home in the evening without getting care. He also has known them to die at home without care. But let him describe the elderly's problems:

Their problem is that they need a family physician to make house calls. In an emergency at night or even during the day it is very difficult to get a doctor to the home. They can't get them unless they can pay fifteen or twenty-five dollars. All my people are on a tight budget from Social Security, maybe a little assistance from welfare, and they cannot afford this. So therefore they must get a neighbor or a friend to call the ambulance to take them to the emergency hospital or ward, and when they are in there they are kept for hours. Sometimes they are turned out at midnight to be sent home, and if they can't get an escort to bring them back they sometimes send the police with them to their home.

Now, many of them live in top-floor rooming houses in the rear, unlighted, no facilities for cooking or food. They are brought home and left alone. We really should have somebody to follow this up, either the nurse's aides or volunteers to follow this up and see how the people are doing, because often they die after they are sent home from the hospital for lack of care.

The experiences in the clinics are the same as I have heard other people say. They are overcrowded, hours of waiting. Sometimes the medical records are misplaced. And there is the problem of getting prescriptions filled at night at the drug counter at the hospital, because there is a big line there all the time. And, of course, I found out that in practically every hospital I visited they all have to wait, and these older people, besides being old, are sick, and it is irritating for them to stand in line and wait and go from one clinic to the other expecting to be able to get out in a minute and they are there for four or five hours sometimes.

The fact is that the elderly and the disabled can simply fade into the background of neglect in our cities when they are too weak to seek out care. Health care in most cases simply will not come to them. As you get older, weaker, and less able to pound at the doors of the health care system, you frequently get less and less attention, even though you need more care than when you were younger.

SEEKING OUT HEALTH CARE IN AN AMBULANCE

If you have a doctor or a hospital to go to, how do you get there?

The last resort is a taxi or an ambulance in emergencies. We heard from people of modest income who must regularly spend large sums for cab fares. Mrs. Berna Kaiser, who lives outside Nashville, must pay twenty-one dollars cab fare twice a month to reach her physician. Residents of small rural communities in West Virginia told of paying a neighbor with a car three, five or ten dollars out of meager incomes to take them to the doctor.

Many people must resort to an ambulance. Americans seem frequently to view the ambulance as the long arm of the physician or the hospital reaching out to them in emergencies. Unfortunately, this is seldom true. In most cities and counties, the hospitals and the physicians take no responsibility for making sure the ambulances are properly equipped or the attendants properly trained. Nor do they make any effort to insure that the service is fast or responsive to emergencies. The physician's and the hospital's responsibility begins only when you reach their door. The ambulance is not their way of reaching out to the patient in an emergency—it is simply a tool the patients can use to seek out the physician.

Frequently the services are operated by people who know nothing about health care. Dr. Joseph Bistowish, director of health for metropolitan Nashville and Davidson County, described the ambulance service operated there by funeral homes.

DR. BISTOWISH: All of our ambulance service is furnished by funeral directors. Attendants on these ambulances have, for the most part, little or no training for their work. Equipment carried on the ambulances is inadequate. There is no provision for exchange of equipment between ambulances and emergency rooms so that ambulances will not be unduly delayed at hospitals. There are no standing orders as to where certain types of injuries will be taken for emergency room service. . . .

There is no system of radio communication between ambulances and emergency rooms so there could be advance warning given to the emergency room to get certain equipment ready. There is no dispatch service available to avoid two or three ambulances showing up at the same time.

SENATOR KENNEDY: Suppose you had radio equipment, would it make a difference in terms of saving lives?

DR. BISTOWISH: Yes, it would even make it possible for a physician on duty in the hospital to give information to the attendant on the scene for a particular type of injury. . . .

There was a newspaper account some time ago in which two ambulances arrived at the scene of an accident and the drivers argued over which one would take the corpse while leaving the injured person unattended on the ground. Approximately two years ago a group of teenagers had an automobile accident almost in the front yard of a local physician. Because of the type of injury to one of the youngsters, this physician recommended to the ambulance driver that the patient be taken to a particular hospital. The driver let the physician know in no uncertain terms that he made the decision as to where the patient would be taken.

In Cleveland, the ambulance service is operated by the city police department. Mrs. Arthur Woods described her experiences with this service.

MRS. WOODS: I would like to cite one case out of four that I was definitely involved in, one case on July 20, 1969, when my husband died. The police were called at ten minutes to twelve, and after three calls, repeated calls, the police finally arrived at twelve-fifteen. At the time I thought my husband had suffered a heart attack. An autopsy, though, revealed that he had died from a massive cerebral hemorrhage, but neither I nor the police knew that at the time.

I live at 1937 East Eighty-ninth Street, which is only a few blocks away from the Fifth District Police Department. The police, in not arriving until twelve-fifteen, did not come directly to the house. They parked across the street from the house, evidently afraid of the area and what might happen, since we had had a Glenville incident, and they were very particular about any calls of this sort in the inner city.

When they did finally come into the home—the police had been told, mind you, that my husband had suffered a heart attack, because the telephone operator did call the police department—they did not come up with a cot to take him out, they did not come up with blankets, they came in the house, stepped over my husband and asked me was I married to this man.

And they didn't have a resuscitator either. Well, I was, at the time, giving him artificial respiration and he was still breathing. I said, "Please go down and get the resuscitator, he's still living," And the police said, "Well, I think it's too late now."

I said, "You're not a doctor." And they became very hostile toward me. One finally went down for the resuscitator and came back and . . . asked the other one did he know how to use it, because he didn't. So he didn't get the resuscitator.

On top of everything else, ambulances can be slow and expensive. Mr. Vernon Watkins described the plight of the people of Newberg, West Virginia, in this regard.

MR. WATKINS: I represent the town of Newberg, with a population of about 494 people. About one third of them are retired persons, which I am very interested in, because I am going to be one of those retired persons in a few years. Our medical facilities—we used to have a doctor there about twenty years ago, but we have not had any. We are about fourteen miles from Grafton Hospital, about fourteen miles from Kingwood.

Our old people are the most important people we have today. They are stepped on in about every way. They don't have the income, as we have heard it told here today. Most of them have incomes of around eighty to a hundred dollars a month, and to try to keep a house on it and electric and telephone, to try to get somebody to take them to a doctor, it is hard.

Our public transportation in Preston County is worse today than it was forty years ago. We used to get Kingwood public transportation thirty or forty years ago, and today you can't —in Newberg, or most any place in the county. We have one bus line that runs from Oakland to Morgantown and that is about it. Everybody, if he doesn't have a car, just about walks today.

We are one of largest counties in the state, strung out over these hills and hollows, you might say. We have an ambulance service in this county which is inadequate today. We have two ambulances serving the whole county.

I am in the coal mines. I am director of safety for a coal mine. I had to set up a plan to get men to the hospital as quick as possible. This service just started the first of March. I am not taking anything away from the people that run the ambulance. But it takes thirty minutes to get to Newberg, which is fourteen miles. I checked with an accident we had down there last week, and also about two to three weeks ago, [when] we had a man who had a stroke and the ambulance was called at fifteen after three. [It] came to the home at around four or four-fifteen. By the time they got him to the hospital, it was five o'clock and the doctor had already left. They called the doctor and he stayed awhile and left because he thought the man had died on the road or something, and the doctor had to be called back out again.

Other residents of rural West Virginia described how the private ambulance companies demanded cash in hand when they arrived; without cash on the spot they would not take anyone to the hospital. Even at that, the rural private company had trouble staying in business. One lady at our West Virginia hearing, Mrs. Hill, stood and shouted from the audience about ambulance services.

MRS. HILL: Before they came out and do anything, you have to have cash money for them. If it is a welfare patient, they still have to have the cash.

SENATOR KENNEDY: Before they will take you?

MRS. HILL: It costs about thirty-six dollars to come from Morgantown, for a one-hour trip.

SENATOR RANDOLPH: Who made the ambulance trip? Who operated the ambulance?

MRS. HILL: They ask you before they go if you have the money to pay them. You have to have cash. When they brought my grandmother home, we had to have the cash ready or they wouldn't have gone after her and picked her up.

Lack of transportation and adequate ambulance services represents yet another way in which it is left to the people to seek out health care. Health professionals won't come to them, nor do they take an active responsibility for seeing that arrangements made to bring people to the doctor's or hospital's door are best in terms of their health care.

PLACES DOCTORS REFUSE TO GO

Perhaps the most difficult problem of seeking out a doctor is faced by those who live in rural counties that simply cannot attract physicians to provide them with health care. Some counties go to extreme efforts to make themselves attractive to a physician. In West Virginia, a pharmacist, a lawyer and a local businessman described their efforts to attract a physician to Doddridge County.

MR. HOWARD SPURLOCK: We are from Doddridge County, which is a rural area of less than seven thousand people. We also live in a small town under twelve hundred. The economy is based on textile factory, oil and gas production, farming and cattle raising.

In the spring of 1966, the Sears, Roebuck Foundation's Aid to Rural Areas (by providing increased medical facilities) was contacted and asked to make a survey of our basic medical needs. After the survey, it was determined that this county could very easily support three physicians. And we should prepare for the future by building a medical facility. We started a fund drive of $50,000, and this was all private money. There was no government money involved. It came from the citizens. We concluded this January 1, 1967. Afterwards we added another $30,000 in medical equipment. Prior to this, we did have one physician servicing the whole county. He was sixty-two years of age and had decided to leave.

We had a public meeting with the Sears Foundation in 1966, and at that time they gave us the impression that with this modern facility we would be able to find us another doctor or two, as the clinic was built to take care of two physicians. In September of 1967 we opened the clinic, and we did have a foreign graduate physician and an American lady pediatrician. They came in September 1967 and they left in April of 1968. We spent the next six months pursuing all possibilities of getting another physician for the county.

SENATOR RANDOLPH: Why did they leave?

MR. SPURLOCK: One had immigration problems, and the

lady pediatrician was following her husband, who was a music professor and moved on.

We managed to get another foreign graduate in November of '68. He stayed until November of '69. He left. He had immigration problems. So that leaves us where we are now, without a doctor. In the last forty months we have had a doctor for nineteen months. This means that we have been without basic medical facilities for our citizens, and our citizens are welfare and also middle-class, and these are the people that can pay a bill but cannot get the services.

We are thirty-five minutes away from hospital facilities. We have sent people in an ambulance into Clarksburg and we have had people die on the way in, and immediate medical attention could have saved some of these people. So we are up a tree. We have tried everything we now know to get a physician. We have advertised in periodicals, medical journals, newspapers, we sent out 120 letters to medical universities all over the country and Army discharge centers. We haven't had a direct reply from any of these. We have had people come in, but for one reason or another they didn't want to locate there.

SENATOR RANDOLPH: Are you speaking now of the county as a whole?

MR. SPURLOCK: I am speaking of the county as a whole. We have no doctor from one end to the other. We are really thirty-five minutes away from medical care.

SENATOR RANDOLPH: Mr. Spurlock, you know the problem in Clay County?

MR. SPURLOCK: I read about it.

SENATOR RANDOLPH: There is a nonprofit organization that has been formed there where they will guarantee the salary of the physician, if he will come, $36,000 a year, the dentist $23,000 a year, and the pharmacist $18,000 a year, and provide $4,000 for an inventory with which the pharmacist can open his shop, as it were. This is a rather unusual effort that is being made there. I don't know whether it will succeed or not. But there is no doctor in that county, just as there is no doctor in your county.


Doddridge County, West Virginia, is not alone in its plight. There are five other counties near Doddridge County with no doctor, and other such counties in rural states all over the country. Mr. Howard Sheets, a pharmacist in Afton, Iowa, described efforts to attract a physician almost identical to those made by Mr. Spurlock.

In addition, there are many, many more rural communities which have some doctors—but which are losing physicians faster than they can be replaced. For example, in Kingwood, the principal town of Preston County, West Virginia, there were ten family physicians one year ago. In the last year, two died and one left for a residency in neurosurgery. None has been replaced. Today there are seven; of these, five are over fifty, two are over forty-five. Even counting the retired doctor, two specialists, and two physicians employed by a state hospital in the county, this means there is one doctor for every 2,250 people in the county surrounding Kingwood. Compare this to the national average of one doctor for every 632 people. Some suburban areas such as Westchester County of New York, a suburb of New York City, enjoy one physician for four hundred people.

There is a hospital in Kingwood, West Virginia, whose dedicated administrator struggles to attract nursing and other staff. Miss Iris Allsopp pointed out how hard it is to compete for these staff people with industrialized urban areas. One wing of this fine hospital is closed, padlocked. Roughly one third of its beds are sealed off, and the rest of the hospital has a utilization rate of about fifty percent. Superficially, there is simply no demand.

On the contrary, Dr. Delroy Davis, who practices in Kingwood and heads the Preston County Medical Society, suggested that there was a need for more care in the county, that many of the poor and their children don't get the preventive care they need such as Pap smears and immunizations. He suggested that the county, which has 25,000 residents, could use four or five more doctors.

Dr. Davis suggested that if there were more doctors the hospital in Kingwood might be full. Counting the closed ward, there are a total of seventy-six beds available in Kingwood for 25,000 people in the county. The national average for community hospitals is 4.2 beds per 1,000 population. Given these averages, Kingwood could use over a hundred beds. The padlocked ward in Kingwood might well be used if there were doctors and other staff to serve the county.

But you don't have to use statistics to reach this conclusion. We went into the small towns and hollows around Kingwood and we saw the need for health care. We saw the children with obvious health problems; we heard mothers describing their long journeys to a university clinic for care; we heard the elderly describe their lack of transportation to get to the doctor; we heard the reports of a team of students who ventured into these areas to test and treat children for intestinal worms. We visited others who did not understand their need for care or feared being mocked in the city. All worried over how they could pay.

The need for health care is there in Kingwood, but there aren't enough doctors even to treat the people who seek out health care, much less to go out looking for work. What a contrast to the Westchester Counties of America with their oversupply of physicians. The head of a sophisticated group of physicians in Mount Kisco, an affluent community in Westchester County, described much of the illness they treated as "inconsequential." "This is luxury medicine," he said.

Yet, in the face of this uneven distribution, most graduates of medical schools in rural states leave their state to practice in urban areas. In a meeting with one group of such students, most of whom were born in the state, I was told that they knew they could make $40,000 a year wherever they go. That being the case, they chose to go to the cities, where they and their families could have the social and cultural advantages their education had taught them to appreciate.

The ease with which this decision can be made is doubly troublesome when one stops to consider that medical education in many rural states is heavily subsidized by taxes collected by the state. West Virginia, for example, contributed over $3 million to its medical school in 1969, but has retained only twenty-nine percent of its graduates to practice medicine in the state. Yet the people of West Virginia are among the poorest in per-capita income. Residents of such rural states have helped pay for the education of physicians practicing "luxury medicine" in places like Westchester County.

There are dedicated physicians like Dr. Davis in many rural areas; we were especially impressed with the social conscience displayed by osteopaths in Iowa and with efforts of such institutions as Broadlawns Hospital in Des Moines to train family physicians and encourage them to practice in rural Iowa. But there just aren't enough physicians, dentists, nurses, and other health professionals willing to seek out the people who need their help the most.

Nor are the rural areas alone in this plight. The hearts of

America's great cities are also critically short of physicians. One reason city hospitals are being swamped with patients in their emergency rooms and outpatient clinics is that there are too few doctors outside the hospital to care for them. In New York City, according to Dr. John L. S. Holloman, two thirds of the people must get care from only one third of the physicians. There are 150 physicians serving 223,000 people in central Harlem—one of every 1,600 people. Yet, a few miles away there are over 4,000 physicians on expensive Park Avenue and its side streets.

The fact is that with some exceptions members of the health care professions, like the members of other professions, go where they like the style of life and can be assured of the best income. Neither the government nor any other institution intervenes to get physicians where they are needed most.

It is inconvenient that automobile dealers tend to migrate toward the suburbs, leaving rural and inner-city residents at a disadvantage for getting maintenance service. But it is tragic and unacceptable for physicians and hospitals to leave areas of the country without adequate health care.

Actually, the automobile dealer and most other businesses work to attract their customers to them, or they go to seek their customers out. They have to in order to make a living. Not so the health professional. Since he can make a good income no matter where he practices, he can set up shop wherever it suits him, without concern for where the people need him most. The people must seek him out—he won't seek them out.

## MY CONVICTION

*The health care system should seek out the people who need care. People who are injured, sick and frightened should not have to pound at the system's doors, overcoming obstacles, to reach health care. Health care should be given to those who need it, not just to those who are fortunate enough to live where the doctors are, aggressive enough to insist on and arrange care, and affluent enough to pay for transportation and treatment.*

*It is not acceptable to allow some areas of our country to go without adequate health care because they are not professionally, culturally, or financially attractive to health care professionals. Nor is it acceptable to leave the disabled, the elderly, and the uninformed without help until they reach the hospital's or the doctor's door.*

*If we continue to act as if the provider's responsibility begins when the patient comes to his door, we will never get enough physicians into these shortage areas in our country, nor will we ever get adequate health care to these millions of Americans with special needs. In the "seller's market" that exists in health care, a provider can get enough patients to come to his door to support a handsome salary almost anywhere in the country. The provider therefore has little incentive to enter areas or offer services he considers less attractive and less profitable.*

*Moreover, it may be acceptable for auto mechanics, plumbers, or other service professions to build obstacles to keep people's demands from disrupting their personal lives, but when human suffering is at stake it is unacceptable to build obstacles to health care.*

*America should change the ground rules of health care to require that doctors, hospitals, and others remove all obstacles to care and that they actively seek out Americans who need health care. We should place this burden on the health system, but also take every possible step to assure health care professionals a sane life at a fair income in professionally rewarding surroundings.*

*I believe we can accomplish this through an enlightened national health insurance program such as I describe in the last chapter.*

CHAPTER V

# The Medical Maze

AN American today may find himself suspended among a dozen or more individuals or organizations who deal with health care. There are the doctors and dentists and the hospitals, laboratories, and nursing homes that provide care; and the insurance companies and the federal Social Security or state and county offices which are supposed to help arrange or pay for his family's health care.

If an American itemizes medical deductions for his family on his income-tax return, he may well find he can claim all of the following.

- Payments to several drugstores for prescription drugs.
- Payments to one or more health insurance companies.
- Payments to one or more hospitals for hospitalization.
- Payments to laboratories or hospitals for laboratory work.
- Payments to doctors. These may include:
    the family physician or internist
    the pediatrician
    the obstetrician

    the dentist
    the dental surgeon
    the orthodontist
    the general surgeon
    the ophthalmologist
    other specialists.
He may also record payments for:
    special nursing care
    psychiatric consultations
    special medical supplies or equipment
    ambulance services.

Each of these organizations and individuals acts as an independent business. Each specialist and each institution of our medical care system is geared to a particular kind of illness, while no one shows concern for the overall health care of an individual. The system does not organize itself around the individual to offer preventive care, nor does it adequately organize around him to meet his health needs if he falls ill. Each one of the specialists and institutions frequently assumes that his individual responsibility begins and ends when the person crosses his doorstep.

Most physicians are in solo practice in America or in practice with other physicians of the same specialty. If you need the services of another specialist, one physician may refer you to another, but it is up to you to find the recommended physician, make and then wait for an appointment, and get to his office—frequently at some distance. You will also frequently find you have to start from the beginning in describing your health problem, since the first physician won't have called or discussed the case with the new physician or given any of your background. Very likely you will also find that tests and X rays that have already been taken are repeated by the second physician. Even if he is willing to use your earlier tests, there may be no way to get the tests to him short of your arranging it yourself. It is as if each physician is a business in himself, and as if his business ends when you leave his door. The specialist to whom you are referred also thinks of himself as an independent business and is not necessarily concerned with what the other physician did or what happened to you before you came through his door. Neither physician sees it as his business to keep track of the entire course of your care or the total cost to you.

Similarly hospitals, laboratories, nursing homes and other organizations frequently act as independent businesses. A physician may inform a patient that he no longer needs hospital care but needs instead a skilled nursing home. Neither the physician nor the hospital will necessarily see to it that the patient finds and gets to a nursing home. As with physician referrals, the patient may be given a list of names but be left on his own to make all the arrangements.

Financing arrangements are no less difficult. The health insurance salesman is not obliged to describe exactly how his policy fits in with Medicare or with other policies that a person may own or that he might buy if he chose to. In fact, as in many of the cases recounted here, most families have no way of knowing the real value of their insurance until they fall ill. The patient's family is left to figure out what benefits it is entitled to from its various sources of support. If he is hospitalized, he may get help from the hospital in filling out the forms, but if he is surprised or disappointed in the payment he receives from the insurance company it is his job to figure out why it is lower than he expected. The hospital and the physician may help him, but he shouldn't count on it. The insurance is, after all, not part of their business.

Some physicians are better than others at organizing their

practices so that the laboratory, the specialist's office, and other services are nearby and can be reached at minimum cost, inconvenience, and confusion for the patient. Some physicians team up with other doctors of various specialties in a medical center where laboratory facilities are available. The fact remains, however, that there is no obligation for any physician, insurance company, hospital, nursing home, etc., to act like anything but a completely independent business. Most assume no responsibility for the other aspects of health care or for helping the patient through the system at minimum cost and confusion. In fact, most Americans are forced to organize their own health care and their way of paying for it.

Americans must frequently decide for themselves which of many specialists they need, and sometimes they are left to decide between conflicting opinions offered by specialists. They are left to arrange for themselves special nursing, medicines, equipment, or nursing-home care and to determine what financial help they can claim. They are themselves the only ones who know completely even their most recent health care history. Unfortunately, Americans are sometimes left to do these things when they themselves or a member of their family have been weakened by illness or injury. For the elderly, the disabled, and those with limited income and education, this can be an impossible burden.

The question is, who *should* be responsible for making sure Americans find their way successfully from one specialist to another, from the doctor's office to the laboratory, to the hospital, to the nursing home? Who should help a family plan its coverage, and who figures out, after illness has struck, what is covered by insurance, by Medicare benefits, by welfare benefits? Whose responsibility is it to keep a record of a person's history of health care?

The histories that follow dramatize some of the inefficiencies of our fragmented system and the burden that this fragmentation places on the individual to organize his own care.

## FRAGMENTATION OF SERVICES AMONG SPECIALISTS

The story related by Mr. Dale Gentz, a member of a Los Angeles hospital's administrative staff, illustrates some of the problems of coordinating referrals among doctors in various medical specialties.

Mr. Gentz's wife, Maxine, saw five physicians. The first attempted extensive treatment before calling in a specialist. The second and third, who are orthopedic surgeons, repeated much of this treatment before asking for tests and advice from a neurologist. The neurologist apparently decided to approach it in his own way and never reported anything. The fifth physician, another neurologist, did perform the tests and offer the advice requested. When surgery was performed, Mr. Gentz feels, the surgeon in effect split the fee with the physician who originally referred Mrs. Gentz to him.

One can't help but wonder if the cost and the anguish would not have been less if each specialist had been working as part of a team, rather than running his own solo business and attempting to solve the problem on his own.

But let Mr. Gentz tell the story.

MR. GENTZ: My story is about my wife, Maxine. It began about a year ago last month, when she developed a back problem—low-back pain, which apparently is not an uncommon situation among the population. And she sought medical treatment from our local M.D., who put her in the hospital and put her in traction, prescribed therapy, whirlpool therapy, ultrasound therapy, pain medications, muscle relaxants—the whole gamut of conservative therapy. He did X rays; found nothing.

She did not improve, and they sent her home to continue basically the same things on an outpatient basis. For the next five months she lived on pain medications and muscle relaxants, neither of which did any good. He finally became fed up and referred her to an orthopedic specialist. He felt whatever was wrong was out of his hands.

The orthopedic specialist repeated a lot of what was done previously, and this was at a duplicate cost. . . . He found very little wrong with her and prescribed an orthopedic corset, which he told her to wear as long as she could tolerate it, which was about one week. This cost us $102.50.

She continued on with more pain medications and more muscle relaxants for the next five months, [until] she was unfortunate enough to fall and reinjure her back even more. She was admitted to the hospital at that time, and the doctor who admitted her said, "I am aware of your case and I think it is about time we tried to find out what is the problem."

This was eight, nine months after she first started going to the doctor. She was seen by another orthopedic specialist, because we were unhappy with what we received from the first one. And the specialist gave her a myelogram and found nothing. He kept her in the hospital for two weeks and got nowhere.

She was discharged from the hospital at the end of January and scheduled to see a neurologist for an electromyelogram to determine possible nerve involvement. . . . She saw the neurologist, who didn't do what the specialist requested. Not only did he not do it, but he didn't get the report out to our doctor. And about a month went by and she was readmitted to the hospital. The doctor called in another neurologist at a duplicate cost, after never having received the information from the first one. They repeated—they did the test which had not been done the first time, and they found what they thought was a herniated lumbar disc. At that time they scheduled her for surgery and sent her home, because surgery couldn't be scheduled for a couple of days.

She came home for two days and was readmitted to the hospital and she had surgery. Fortunately for her now, ten weeks later, she finally had a good day. She felt very well Sunday. This is the first time in about fourteen months. . . .

During that time she has incurred almost $8,000 worth of medical bills for this alone. That, I think, is a part of the problem. I have the good fortune, I guess, of having hospitalization. . . .

I now owe about $1,200, and don't really have any idea how I am going to be able to pay this bill. The bills are distributed over several different places—one hospital with three bills, a total of about $600, and three doctors, each of whom are demanding immediate payment. . . .

SENATOR KENNEDY: You work in a hospital, do you not?

MR. GENTZ: Yes, sir. I do. I am on the administrative staff of a major teaching hospital in southern California.

SENATOR KENNEDY: So you probably have as much familiarity with or understanding of how the system functions and works as perhaps anyone.

MR. GENTZ: Yes, sir. I certainly do. . . .

SENATOR KENNEDY: And if you had been able to receive the best kind of advice in the beginning, you would have saved yourself, your family, the pain and suffering and hardship which you have endured.

MR. GENTZ: That's correct, yes, sir. It became fairly clear after about three months that my wife had a problem which was orthopedic. The doctor whom we normally go to for treatment is a general practitioner, which means he has had one year of training beyond his medical school. . . .

My general practitioner was the assistant on the surgery for my wife. Now, this is not unusual. This is common practice. It is perhaps ironic that my orthopedic surgeon has a partner who is also a specialist in orthopedic surgery, yet the assistant was a general practitioner who, again, has only had one year of training beyond medical school. When I found out that approximately forty-five percent of his fee for assisting was not covered by the insurance or by the insurance schedule, I tried to find out why. . . . And what I am about to say, I think, is my own opinion. . . .

What this amounts to is that the doctor has given the general practitioner a sophisticated form of fee-splitting, and he is kicking back to the doctor a "thank you" for referring him a patient. You have no control over that. This is not my first experience with the assistant's fees in surgery and involving my wife. And the first time was a similar situation. When I confronted the doctor he said, "You can't prove I wasn't in the operating room." I saw him at the hospital that day. However, he was fully clothed about two minutes after my wife was brought out of surgery, which makes it difficult for me to believe. But, as he said, I can't prove it. And he had to be there to close if the doctor died on the table, which didn't happen.

It is all very frustrating to run into this kind of thing, particularly when, allegedly, I know the shortcuts. I should know who the people are to contact to get what I want, and I can't.

The case of Mrs. Shizuki Ichiyasu, whose husband injured his back working in a hardware store, further illustrates the problem of fragmentation and of the layman's problem of sorting out differing medical opinions.

Mrs. Ichiyasu, who lives in San Francisco, is a strong woman capable of managing conflicting advice, checking various opinions, and guiding her way among specialists, physiotherapists and others. In this case a fragmented insurance coverage complicated the story, but the question remains: Why could the physicians not have consulted with one another, instead of Mrs. Ichiyasu's having to do it? If the patient's condition had been reviewed by the specialists together, might they not have solved the problem sooner?

MRS. ICHIYASU: It was about eighteen months ago—about eighteen months ago my husband was injured on the job; and at that time he felt it wasn't quite serious, so it didn't incapacitate him in any way.

SENATOR KENNEDY: Where does your husband work?

MRS. ICHIYASU: At a hardware store. Since 1952.

SENATOR KENNEDY: Eighteen, nineteen years.

MRS. ICHIYASU: Not taking it very seriously, he just mentioned it to his employer; but he continued working.

Gradually the discomfort became worse and worse, and finally he decided he had better be examined by a doctor. He was told that since it was an industrial accident he must go to a doctor that was designated by the insurance company. . . . The inference was very strong that if he did not go to the doctor they designated he may end up assuming the full financial responsibility for any expenses that might be incurred. So he went to the doctor, who diagnosed it as bilateral hernia. He had surgery. The doctor's report stated a slight hernia on one side, no hernia on the other.

But after a period of convalescence my husband felt increased discomfort of the back, the left leg. The doctor tried to tell him he had gout at that point. . . . A series of uric tests indicated that he had gout, and therefore this doctor said he would recommend a certain type of medical treatment or medication to correct this situation.

Since it was not related to the injury, my husband felt at this time if he did have gout he would rather be treated by his own personal physician. We consulted our doctor, and he sent my husband for a series of uric-acid tests. The results were completely in contradiction to what the insurance doctor had indicated, so my husband refused to continue the treatment. So this insurance doctor said, at the end of December, "So far as I am concerned, you are ready to go back to work."

SENATOR KENNEDY: Do I understand when he went to the doctor that was recommended by the insurance company he diagnosed it as gout?

MRS. ICHIYASU: Initially it was diagnosed as a bilateral hernia; and when the pain did not go away, he diagnosed it as gout.

SENATOR KENNEDY: When the insurance doctor said it was gout, your husband thought it wouldn't be covered, so he went over to his own doctor and he diagnosed it and said it wasn't gout?

MRS. ICHIYASU: If it was related to his injury, it was covered; but the gout, which is a total medical—

SENATOR KENNEDY: How is your husband supposed to know? If one doctor says he has gout, and the other says he doesn't have it, what is he supposed to do?

MRS. ICHIYASU: He had his personal physician conduct a health examination periodically, and he figures his own doctor knew more about it than a new doctor coming in out of the cold, treating him for another condition. And the lab report was done by another pathologist, not our own internist, and therefore this is two doctors' opinion actually contradicting the gout diagnosis.

The pain persisted, and with much negotiations with the insurance company we finally got them to go along with the idea of having my husband examined by a back specialist, who diagnosed it as some kind of muscle injury related to the back. He had physiotherapy for about two months, during which time the condition worsened, and the doctor at least was honest to report that he was no longer able to help my husband, and so he was referred back to the insurance company, who, in turn, contacted a neurosurgeon.

SENATOR KENNEDY: I am sorry to interrupt. Your husband has been told he has a hernia and gout and a muscle sprain by three different doctors, is that right?"

MRS. ICHIYASU: No—the hernia and gout was one doctor. He has enough doctors without adding any more.

SENATOR KENNEDY: Two doctors and three opinions.

MRS. ICHIYASU: He was hospitalized, after various tests— electromyelograms and so forth. They determined it was disc damage.

May first he had surgery done. Immediately after, they noticed that there was some infection which they weren't able to pinpoint to any other cause and the reports indicated that it possibly was related to the back surgery, although there was no visible sign of that as far as X rays and tests were concerned.

He was put in a body cast, in which he remained for about two months. Most of the time he spent at home. Now, if you visualize the body cast from, say from the chest down to, almost down to the knees, you realize that a man is not able to sit. For his meals, he would have to stand.

In order to go to the hospital to have the cast removed and have further evaluation we had to rent a car, in which he could recline.

He had the cast removed, had other tests done, evaluations —and he was discharged, and from the late summer to December of 1970 he remained at home.

We had a physical therapist come to the house for a couple of weeks. The treatment was very minimal and the results were absolutely nil, so he explained to the doctor that he didn't think it was helping him any.

In December he was hospitalized again, for further evaluation, and discharged. And from January through March he went to a physiotherapist twice a week. And from March the insurance company indicated they had wanted him to go every day, but the doctor—this is the insurance doctor— said this was too much and suggested trying three times. Up through April 9 he was going thrice weekly .

The following Monday, he was admitted to the hospital for psychotherapy because they felt that possibly some of this was psychologically induced; they said there was probably nothing physically wrong with him any more than due to the depression and things of that nature. And he was not getting along well; he didn't get along with the medicines, and there was a fight for about ten days after he was abruptly discharged. All medication was suddenly cut off, and out of desperation I consulted my own doctor, who recommended we taper off the drugs.

After ten days at home, he developed bladder and lung congestion, I feel after too much drugs. By then he had lost forty pounds and wasn't eating— [Emotionally upset.]

SENATOR KENNEDY: Now, you just take your time, Mrs. Ichiyasu.

MRS. ICHIYASU: I consulted my own doctor and he said it

sounded like a very serious medical condition, but he said it is all related to his original condition and the fact that he was not able to get well. So he suggested I call the insurance doctor. And in turn this doctor was very good about it and said, "Knowing your husband, I feel that you have more confidence if your own doctor were called in." And at his recommendation the insurance company called in our own doctor, who, in turn, called in a urologist—the urologist—and things of that nature.

He was admitted Friday, April 30. He was extremely violent, and they thought that he would have to be institutionalized. By midmorning Saturday he was comatose and they found a lung infection and things of that nature. So, realizing it was a critical medical condition brought on by all this, our doctor started the proper treatment, and after two weeks of hospitalization he came home with the acute medical problems corrected. . . .

He is home now and he is still in bed, and the doctor was out yesterday and he said that we will see what transpires. So I asked him to see if they could follow up on the neurologist's report and get the insurance company to not wait so long and take some definite action so that they can get my husband on the mend for a change.

### SOLO PRACTICE AND SPECIALIZATION
### CONTRIBUTE TO FRAGMENTATION

Mr. Gentz and Mrs. Ichiyasu described extreme and difficult cases. Most Americans, however, experience the frustrations of fragmentation of services among specialists.

"My bursitis seems to be back. The last time my internist gave me a shot, he missed the spot, and sent me to an orthopedic surgeon. He hit it right away. Should I go to the internist or to the orthopedic surgeon this time? It may not be bursitis. But if I go to the internist I have to wait for an appointment with him, and then may have to wait again for the surgeon—*and pay twice.* I wonder if the internist knows what the surgeon found last time when he took an X ray? But then, the surgeon may not think of other things that might be wrong. Mother's arm hurt when she had her heart atack."

This is a hypothetical case. But I'll wager every reader has pondered such factors during any number of illnesses in his family and has had to decide. I believe physicians could organize themselves in this country to minimize such problems.

As specialization increases, the need to organize specialists into teams increases. The patient should not have to organize doctors or endure repeated examinations, tests, and the possibility of divergent opinions. There has to be some point where overall responsibility lies. Right now for the vast majority of Americans that is the patient, and only the patient. The problem is that the patient is not qualified or capable of organizing the physicians. They should organize themselves.

One of the primary contributions to fragmentation of care is the strong custom of solo-practice medicine and the increasing trend toward specialization among physicians. Of the 278,500 practicing physicians in the United States in 1970, a large majority were in solo practice and 220,000 were specialists rather than general practitioners. Of the relatively few in group practice (40,000 in 1969), many were in groups which represented only one specialty.

The trend toward specialization has been rapid in recent years. In 1970 there were 58,000 physicians in general practice, compared to 73,000 in 1963, a loss of 15,000 in seven years. It is difficult to find general practitioners in most areas. Dr. Delroy Davis in Kingwood, West Virginia, described his efforts to get a family practitioner to share a practice:

Experience in looking for a partner in family practice this past year has brought approximately one hundred applications from specialists, mostly surgeons who would be willing to do general practice until they could do their specialty. We received only four inquiries from general physicians. I believe this illustrates the deficiency in the curriculum of the medical schools in not training general physicians.

The combination of solo practice (or single-specialty group practice) and specialization contribute heavily to the fragmentation of physician services. They mean more and more separate "one-man businesses" with which the patient must deal to get health care. Earlier in our history, an American went to this family doctor, who usually practiced alone, for all of his care. As medicine has progressed and medical specialties have developed, doctors have clung to the traditions of solo practice, leaving the patient to find his way among many doctors of many different specialties in many different offices.

It would seem more logical in many ways for the solo-practice physician to be replaced by groups representing all the basic specialties who practice together and consult with one another, bringing together their more extensive knowledge in each specialty around the patient's problems. Certainly such a pattern of practice is more helpful to the patient.

FRAGMENTATION AMONG INSTITUTIONS

Why must a fifty-six-year-old man who has been ill, cannot talk, and lives alone be sent out to locate an equipment store and rent several pieces of equipment whose quality he cannot judge but on which he depends for his life? A letter was sent to the public-health nurse, but she was several days away by mail, working for the government. Isn't it possible for the hospitals, the equipment suppliers, and the public-health nurses to be more closely organized around the needs of the patient?

These were the questions raised in my mind in Des Moines, Iowa, by the story of Roy Tillery. Mrs. Joanne Williams, a public-health nurse, brought Mr. Tillery, a rate clerk for a trucking firm, to our hearing and described how fragmentation of services almost cost him his life.

MRS. WILLIAMS: I was asked to come with Mr. Tillery to be able to speak for him, and I will try to do just that, letting him answer questions in writing that you might have, and I will read those to you. I do that since Mr. Tillery had a total laryngectomy last month. . . . Mr. Tillery was operated on in Iowa City on the tenth of April this year. . . . Mr. Tillery, after having the laryngectomy, returned home to Des Moines on the twenty-sixth of April, and this is where problems begin, particularly in the area of funds. To have the kind of care that is needed to care for this surgery that he has had requires some special equipment. These things, the main items, would be a humidifier that is crucial for him to have in his home at all times, and a tracheal suction.

He was asked to go to a local agency to obtain the humidifier and the suction that he needed. He followed through with this and did bring home a humidifier, but he did not bring home the suction. He was told that this would have to be rented, and no help was offered in getting that for him.

When we saw him following this, we found that Mr. Tillery had to go to the hospital as an emergency patient. He was taken there by the fire department because he couldn't breathe, and the reason that he couldn't breathe was because—well, two reasons: he hadn't had a suction to do the kind of suctioning that he had been instructed to do, and he had a humidifier that he had obtained, but this humidifier worked so poorly he might as well not have had one. . . .

SENATOR KENNEDY: Now, how in the world does somebody know where to go to get a humidifier and suction? Do they know where to go?

MRS. WILLIAMS: He had some names of places.

SENATOR KENNEDY: Do they give you a list of places and put you on your own?

MRS. WILLIAMS: Yes, and he was trying to follow through with this and, of course, when you go where you are instructed to go and you don't get what you need, then you are blocked, and that's what happened to him. And the fact that he is alone— It was very fortunate that when this happened to him, this emergency arose—it was very early in the morning, about six or seven in the morning—that he was able to arouse someone else in the building. The gentleman whom he did get awake said at first he just didn't want to go to the door this early in the morning and somebody knocking, and he said, "Who's there?," and nobody answered and he just almost didn't go to the door. Of course, if he had not, Mr. Tillery undoubtedly would have died.

SENATOR KENNEDY; Now, what's the cost for renting this kind of equipment?

MRS. WILLIAMS: Twenty dollars a month. That doesn't sound like a lot, but when you don't have any money coming in, you have got that plus bills for doctor's office visits. . . . And Mr. Tillery being a very conscientious man about his bills, this bothers him, you know. He showed me he's got one bill already, and they will, of course, be continuing, and this is a concern. . . .

SENATOR KENNEDY: Has he had some savings over the period of thirty-one years?

MRS. WILLIAMS: Some savings. A little.

SENATOR KENNEDY: How long does he think the savings can last, given this kind of—

MRS. WILLIAMS: Maybe two or three months. . . . Without any income coming in. And he, of course, will later begin some training for his speech, but this you cannot begin right away.

SENATOR KENNEDY: How did you become involved in this case?

MRS. WILLIAMS: This was through referral from Iowa City, and we were pleased that he was referred to us. . . .

SENATOR KENNEDY: How much time had elapsed from the time he had been dismissed from the hospital until the time of your referral?

MRS. WILLIAMS: Just two days, but all this happened so quickly.

SENATOR KENNEDY: All this happened in two days. . . . How old is Mr. Tillery?

MRS. WILLIAMS: Fifty-six. That's still, you know, a young man, but he could retire.


The experience of the parents of six-year-old Allen Roby, which was also recounted to us in Des Moines, is not unusual.

We heard of many cases where hospitals discharged patients in need of nursing care without concern for how the patient would be cared for outside. If the utilization review committee finds that a Medicare patient's improvement no longer requires hospitalization, Medicare payments cease, and the hospital and family find themselves under great pressure to discharge the patient, even though regular nursing care is required. One witness testified to calling eighteen nursing homes in West Virginia on behalf of one such patient.

The Robys' daughter Angie, a registered nurse, told their story.

MISS ROBY: I am speaking on behalf of my parents, who really didn't feel they could go through this themselves.

They had a six-year old child who—it will be three years this April—had been a fairly normal child. He had a mild cerebral palsy, which only really affected him from his elbow down. He was classified as an epileptic, but yet he was a very intelligent child, which showed even when he was in kindergarten, so we felt very happy even though he had this limited cerebral palsy. We thought, well, it could be worse.

Well, on a Tuesday in April it struck. He had a seizure which we thought was a regular seizure. We took him to the hospital, but he never came out of the coma. One week later on a Sunday Dr. —— was called in and he decided the child needed a blood exchange. This didn't help. He did a craniotomy and tracheotomy. [The child] was still living, but still it didn't help.

My parents, after two or three months, took him to Rochester in hopes that the tumor they found during the craniotomy could be removed. They spent a week to a week and a half up in Rochester to no avail. . . .

During this same summer of June, July and August, both my parents and one of my brothers were admitted to Lutheran Hospital. They just couldn't take it any longer because they had all been so close to little Allen, so we had bills pile up from psychiatric care for my mother and my brother.

[Allen] was readmitted to Mercy Hospital—up until September. Then we got a letter from the Utilization Committee saying they could no longer take care of this child, he didn't need hospital services. He was just taking up a bed.

SENATOR KENNEDY: What's the Utilization Committee?

MISS ROBY: As far as I know, they eliminate unnecessary patients to keep the flow of beds open.

SENATOR KENNEDY: What do you mean by that? . . . What sort of unnecessary patients do they eliminate?

MISS ROBY: Well, what I got from one of the doctors was, if they didn't use X rays and didn't need the facilities that are right there in the hospital, like if they needed custodial care, then they really didn't need a hospital, even though we had insurance that would have covered the child for two years. Yet we couldn't bring this child home, we felt, because of the situation with my mother and brother.

SENATOR KENNEDY: So the Utilization Committee said the boy had to leave?

MISS ROBY: He had to leave, right.

SENATOR KENNEDY: In spite of the fact of the conditions in your home?

MISS ROBY: Right, and, you know, they weren't going to be out of any money either. . . .

In November we did bring him home, because we had nowhere else to go. My parents had to take out a $5,000 loan to help with the cost to bring him home. We were told that we had to have a bedroom downstairs, because they didn't feel this child should be carried upstairs and carried back or left upstairs by himself. . . . He had to have a suction for a while, and all these things added to the cost. Besides, we had to have special diapers made and gowns to fit him.

We had him home until the middle of February. He was [then] readmitted to Methodist Hospital for reevaluation, and he had pneumonia. . . . He was there twenty days for the reevaluation and [then] they sent a Utilization Committee letter saying he no longer needed hospital services, he needed custodial care. So they took him to a convalescent home. After about a month or a month and a half my mother got a call saying they would have to remove him, come and get him that day. He was dismissed. It was rainy, it was cold. My mother assumed that the doctor had ordered it, because he had given the order for the child to go to the convalescent home.

We got him home, and two or three days later he was running a temperature. He was developing pneumonia again. She called the doctor. He was very surprised. He didn't even know the child had been dismissed.

SENATOR KENNEDY: The doctor didn't know?

MISS ROBY: No, he didn't. So then we had him home, and he was readmitted only after going to welfare—this was the only way we could get him readmitted to the convalescent home until we could find a foster home because it was a tremendous burden on my parents. They couldn't afford the cost. It was mounting. They were spending seventy-five to a hundred dollars just on doctor bills, medicine and supplies that were needed for him, and yet welfare will not pay or help you in your home. My father had a job at Firestone where he made good money, but yet he still had the $5,000 loan and hospital expenses that were partially left over, and doctor bills.

SENATOR KENNEDY: And eight other children?

MISS ROBY: Right. So eventually we got him back in the convalescent home temporarily until a foster home could be found, and welfare told us if we could find one and they approved it, he could go. Well, we found one. The woman was too old, they were going to retire her. We found another. They had one total-care child already and they would not allow them to take another one.

Our sources were beginning to be exhausted and then we got a call, on the birthday of my little brother, that he would be dismissed in a couple days by the administrator again.

SENATOR KENNEDY: Didn't they know you were searching, trying to find a foster home?

MISS ROBY: They knew this.

SENATOR KENNEDY: Were you a nurse at this time?

MISS ROBY: Yes, I was.

SENATOR KENNEDY: So you know your way around the health system about as well as anyone?

MISS ROBY: And it does just about as much good as a lay person, really. Our insurance was only paying half of what they paid in the hospital bill. It was $17.50 to the convalescent home. So it was in October that they told my mother that she would have to remove the child in a couple days. . . .

Well, on December twenty-third at 4 A.M. we were called to come and get the child and take him to the hospital. December twenty-fourth he died.

The stories of Roy Tillery and the Robys are alike in this respect. In both cases, the patient or the patient's family is left to try to find the help the hospital says is needed. Once they left the hospital door, its primary responsibility ended, it made only minor efforts to help.

Who is responsible for finding the next step in care and

completing the health care? As things stand today, the patient is responsible. No one else takes any responsibility beyond their doors. In both of these cases, the people who were left the responsibility were barely able to handle it. Mr. Tillery almost died as a result.

## FRAGMENTATION AMONG INSURANCE COVERAGES

Perhaps the most fragmented health institution of all is health insurance. There are so many types of plans and so many companies that the average American is baffled in trying to choose. Many Americans simply get the policy their employer or union offers, and do not try to figure out the coverages. Others buy into "group" plans through clubs, associations, or church organizations. Many who must buy private policies look for and buy "individual" plans as extensive as their budgets will allow. Some who are covered by Medicare or by group policies also buy supplemental policies which take up where their other insurance ends, or which cover some items excluded by their other insurance.

During the course of a family's life the wage earner may work for many different companies, each with a different group policy. At some points between jobs, or while working for himself, he may have private insurance or no insurance at all. When he is sixty-five, he enters an entirely new set of benefits with Medicare. Moreover, as unions negotiate and as insurance companies compete to put together more enticing packages at seemingly better prices, the group coverages change.

It is little wonder that most Americans are surprised when they see their hospital and doctor bills. Most of us do not understand what is covered until then. Most of us aren't in a position to evaluate the worth of various insurance policies until we are hit with a surprising bill.

Fragmentation of insurance coverages is also a problem for the hospitals and doctors. The fact that one form of treatment or one diagnosis may be covered and another not may prejudice choice of treatment. But, just as important, the physician and the hospital are frequently unsure of what is covered at all. They may have to cope with hundreds of different policies. Often they simply send their bill to the patient and let him figure out how to handle it.

As a result of the uncertainties and fragmentation in financing, every story of health care seems also to be a story of worry and choices over costs. The costs and how they can be paid seem to be often in both the patient's and the provider's mind.

One of the ironies of our system of paying for health care in America is that the elderly and the poor, who are in the worst position to understand complicated regulations and coverages, are faced with the most fragmented and complicated coverages of all.

In the little town of Bretz, West Virginia, I talked with Catherine Calcioli about her problems in paying for health care. She has received benefits from no fewer than five different programs in her attempt to live as a widow on a little over fifty-six dollars a month: Medicare, private insurance costing four dollars a month to cover the Medicare deductible, United Mine Workers survivor benefits, a West Virginia drug benefits program, and the black-lung program. She has had to establish her eligibility in several of these and is still fighting to prove that her husband did in fact die of black lung. The social worker who helps Mrs. Calcioli feels she is probably not receiving all the benefits she deserves. Her problem is complicated by her doctor's refusal to fill out the various insurance forms.

As a result of these complicated programs social workers and legal-aid representatives find themselves working to help such Americans obtain the benefits that their own investments or government regulations entitle them to. One organization in Morgantown, the Health Education Advisory Team (HEAT), uses "health advocates" to help people find health care. Mr. Gerald Beallor, a social worker at Montefiore Hospital in New York, said:

The social worker spends untold unnecessary hours patching together separate services with holes in them, with bureaucratic red tape, with requirement of form upon form. And where a patient is in a private or a proprietary hospital or doesn't have a social worker available to help, what can happen to the family because they are not aware of the ways in which eligibility can be determined can be disastrous to that family.

Even when eligibility is established, the complexity of coverages baffles many Americans, who find they are obliged repeatedly to pay for bills which they thought Medicare, Medicaid, their own insurance, or some other program would cover. Some groups, such as migrants and American Indians, find they fall into gaps where there is no coverage at all.

This fragmentation is as much a problem for the providers of care as for the patient. In addition to the complex federal and state programs, there are 1,800 private health insurance carriers, most writing many types of policies. Both patient and providers must cope with the forms, and both can be hurt by fragmented coverages.

## MY CONVICTION

*The American people should not carry so much of the responsibility for organizing their own care. It is tragic that Americans are hurt, suffer needlessly, and pay unnecessarily high bills because of disorganized care. It is doubly tragic that the elderly, the weak, and the poor should be faced with a responsibility that thwarts even younger and more affluent Americans. We should require that physicians, institutions, and financing agents for health care organize themselves to better deliver health care to our people.*

*Physicians should assume responsibility for helping patients between specialists and laboratories at minimum cost and confusion to the patient. This may require some physicians to surrender the custom of solo practice where each individual is a business unto himself in order that Americans have a choice of forms of practice where most of their health needs are taken care of in one place by physicians who consult with one another and organize themselves around the patient's needs.*

*Institutions also should take a responsibility that reaches beyond their doors. Hospitals, laboratories, nursing homes, and pharmacies should be organized for the needs of the patient, not as so many businesses operating independently of one another and not noticing or caring if the patient fails to make it from one such business to another.*

*Financing arrangements should be tied in with physicians and institutions in a way that allows Americans to know what services they can depend on and pay for. The thread of "How much will it cost and will the insurance pay for it?" is woven through all the stories of fragmented care. For the sake of both provider and patient, Americans need clearer, less fragmented insurance coverage that encourages better, less fragmented forms of care. Financing needs to be clear and complete enough so that both provider and patient may get about the business of healing without constant concern over the costs of getting well.*

*I believe a national health insurance program will bring these changes about.*

CHAPTER VI

# Good Care, Poor Care

PERHAPS the most disturbing aspect of the health care crisis in America is the questionable quality of much health care. Even those who can pay the price and who have access to a physician or the hospital may not be getting good health care. This is a most difficult subject to raise fairly, because it is widely acknowledged that American medicine at its best is the finest in the world. Moreoever, trust in the physician is a key ingredient in the doctor–patient relationship cherished by most doctors and patients alike. The issue must nonetheless be raised, because many Americans, both providers and users of health services, are deeply concerned about it.

We have heard testimony that the quality of care varies and that some Americans without realizing it are getting poor medical care. Other Americans are given services, particularly surgery, when there is no need for it, and still others are getting incomplete health services. It is not necessarily a matter of income. Even the affluent receive poor care in many cases.

POOR-QUALITY CARE?

Perhaps the most balanced statement on this subject was made by a physician from the American Academy on Pediatrics at a hearing in Washington on March 24, 1971, on health care for children. I asked Dr. William Weil:

SENATOR KENNEDY: We talked about the quality problem we are facing. Let's talk for a moment about wealthy people. Do those people to whom money is no problem regularly receive quality care for their children?

DR. WEIL: No. I have to concern myself a little bit with living with my fellow practitioners for the rest of my life, but the answer has to be no.

I think that we have quite highly variable kinds of care to those who can afford it. This is variable from city to city and community to community, but I have been literally shocked by getting out into the community hospitals where these people receive their care, and finding an extremely variable level of care to the same class of people.

There are complex reasons for this. There is the time available for a physician to spend on a patient's problem. When there is a community of 300,000 people and eight pediatricians, and they are running every minute trying to get their office load taken care of, they often really don't have the kind of time which is necessary for the complicated and difficult problem.

There is the problem of an opportunity to get away from their practice to get their education updated. When they are in solo practice, who is going to cover for them? Who is going to take care of these people if they want to take a week or month off to get updated? If they want to take part in an educational program, where they will learn as well as teach, how will they find the time? These are difficult problems. We have no way to reimburse them for the time they give us as educators, and we try to involve them because out of this educational role they learn. Currently, we can't afford to pay them.

Education and time are the real problem that the practicing physician faces in keeping his abilities up to date. I don't think there are many physicians who want to give poor care, but the opportunity for them to get to the point where they can give good care, as there ought to be, with the knowledge we have today, is extremely limited. And as a result we see increasing problems, as our physician population ages, of being able to give up-to-the-minute kinds of care.

So having dollars is no guarantee whatsoever of being certain of getting adequate health care.

SENATOR KENNEDY: How can they be assured that they are going to receive high-quality care, even the wealthy people?

DR. WEIL: We have no truth-in-packaging law for medicine, and I am not quite sure how one would write it, but without something of that sort there is no way that I can think of that an individual can be certain that the care he is getting is the optimal that he could have with the funds he has available.

SENATOR KENNEDY: How can you improve on quality?

DR. WEIL: I think one of the ways is something that is beginning to grow, and that is group practice. I think when there are a group of physicians working together to provide care, there is a lot of peer review that is informal. The physician shares his problems with his colleagues, and if he doesn't know, probably somebody else in the group knows, and I think in general that if one could get this information—and I don't have it—one could find that there is a better likelihood of getting quality care in a group setting than in a solo setting.

SENATOR KENNEDY: If those wealthy people to whom money is really no problem can't be assured of getting quality care for their children, you can just imagine what happens to those of more modest income, let alone the poor people of this country. It points up the real crisis that we are facing in terms of quality health care for the children in this country.

DR. WEIL: We are running an antique car in a modern automobile race.

The same variation in the quality noted by Dr. Weil was documented in a study of health services in New York City. In 1964 Dr. Ray E. Trussell, director of Columbia University's School of Public Health and Administrative Medicine, studied medical care given the 500,000 members of the Teamsters' Union in New York City. A group of distinguished physicians reviewed the care given a sample of three hundred teamsters or members of their families. Mr. Frank Fitzsimmons summarized this report for the Health Subcommittee:

Just look at the results of our study:
One in five of the hospital admissions was actually unnecessary.
Twenty of the sixty hysterectomies performed were unnecessary, and another six were highly questionable.
One out of five of the hospitalized patients received poor care, and another one in five received only fair care.
In hospitals with no approved training programs and no accreditation by the Joint Commission, nearly half of the patients received poor care.

In the same hospitals less than a third of the physicians caring for Teamster patients were certified by an American specialty board.

More than half of the thirteen Caesarean sections were questionable.

One in five general surgical cases appeared to have been the victims of unjustifiable delays in performing the surgery.

Those are the conclusions, Mr. Chairman. Now let me tell you about several specific cases. . . .

In one instance of an unnecessary hysterectomy, the patient developed a blood clot six days following discharge, necessitating a second eight-day hospital stay. The surveyor noted that if an unnecessary operation had not been performed in the first place, a second admission would not have been required.

A case judged poor was that of a hospitalized middle-aged man who had complained of stomach pains "off and on" for four months. A great deal of laboratory work was done, but, the surveyor commented, "the massive investigation was on a schoolboy level. It covered the waterfront and never followed through on the intestinal complaints that were the major cause of his admission.

Ironically, the study found that the people involved "overwhelmingly" felt that they had received the best of modern care.

In transmitting this study to the Teamsters' Union, Dr. Trussell said:

The findings pose serious questions to trustees of pension and welfare funds, other organizations and agencies, the professions, government, and the community at large in

New York City as to the wisdom, self-discipline, and ethical conduct on the part of *certain* physicians and hospitals in providing medical and surgical care to your employees and their families. . . . Not only are serious humane and ethical issues raised, but *it is evident that much money is being spent on unnecessary or incompetent* care.

As the findings become known it is very important that the Teamster families and the public at large keep in mind that New York City has a very large number of excellent hospitals and thousands of specialists, qualified by training and experience. The problems portrayed by these studies are concentrated largely in small unaccredited hospitals although there are exceptions to this observation. The challenge before you is one of health education, guidance, and continuing evaluation. The challenge to the community and its responsible agencies is how to assure a more uniformly available high level of service.

The fact is that the quality of care that Americans receive varies greatly, and many Americans are receiving poor medical care.

The story of Mrs. Aurora Rodarte of Los Angeles is an example of this poor quality—and of the tragic consequences to which it may lead.

MRS. RODARTE: About seven months ago my husband had a stroke, seizure, convulsion. I took him to the hospital, here at the General, for observation and treatment to find out what was wrong with him. Well, they kept him three days, and the doctor told me that they couldn't find anything wrong with him except a lot of pressure and he was overworked; to go home. And he gave him a lot of pain killers and about two hundred nerve pills, which I took, because I needed them. And so he told me to bring him back in November for a brain scan.

So then about twenty days later he had another seizure about five in the afternoon. I rushed him to the General. The place was empty for once. It was no traffic—nothing moving. It was really slow. So the doctor comes in and looks at him. My husband used to wear glasses, and the doctor asked me if he was blind from one eye, and I told him no. So he looked him over and went out, and then I asked the doctor, "Well, what is wrong?" And he told me he had a seizure.

Well, maybe I am ignorant, but not that ignorant. I knew he had something. So I told him, "Well, aren't you going to keep him?" Because they had his records there.

He says, "No, we are going to give him an injection, and you take him home to calm him down."

So my husband couldn't sit, because after those seizures he got real weak. So I put him in a wheelchair. Then he started vomiting. The nurse gave him the injection. About half an hour later they took his blood pressure. The doctor disappeared. I was waiting for my brother-in-law to pick me up. [My husband] started vomiting. I couldn't get no help. I couldn't get anybody to give me some assistance. So I just did the best I could, and some doctors near the reception desk asked me if they had already looked at the patient. I said, "Yes, but he is vomiting a lot. Can't you do something?"

Well, one of them says, "Well, I will give you a prescription to go and get at the pharmacist's."

I says, "Well, can't you keep him here? Because I am sure something is wrong with him."

And he says, "Well, if the other doctor says to take him home, take him home."

Well, I took him home. No sooner had I got him home than my husband got another seizure. So after that I wasn't going to bring him back to General, since they didn't want to keep him. So that was a problem. So I called the rescue squad again, and the same ambulance driver went. And so I rushed him to the White Memorial then.

But the injection they had given him at the first hospital, afterward I found out that they were treating him for epileptic seizures. So I asked them, "How can you treat a patient for something that you don't know that he has?" Whatever they gave him, he couldn't come out of that second seizure. He tried, and he was groggy, so he just couldn't. That blindness in his eyes meant that he was getting paralyzed already on one side. He [the first doctor] was supposed to be one of the top neurologists; imagine what the interns could do. That is what made me mad. I told them that it was just malpractice. I mean, if that's the type of care they are going to give in an emergency— You know that when something happens in an emergency, no [private] doctor will touch you. You have to rush him to an emergency hospital. So they told me, "You have a private doctor." Yes, but in an emergency, what are emergency hospitals for? That is what I argued about. They did not give me the care free. The insurance covered it. And I wasn't able to pay the balance, either, not for the care they gave him. Even in his condition they made sure that he had that insurance. They made him sign papers first. I think it is wrong.

SENATOR KENNEDY: What happened to your husband?

MRS. RODARTE: He died.

SENATOR KENNEDY: After—

MRS. RODARTE: About five hours later.

SENATOR KENNEDY: Did you get a bill from the hospital?

MRS. RODARTE: Yes, I gave it back to them. I wasn't about to pay. I didn't sign nothing. My husband signed it. He was dead. I wasn't about to pay, because I don't think in the first place the service they gave him was any service and, after all, they were not doing it free. When I put him in the hospital it was for a complete observation, checkup, and everything.

UNNECESSARY HEALTH SERVICES

Many Americans are confronted with unnecessary pain and discomfort—and with unnecessary expenses—by providers who perform unnecessary services.

Dr. Alex Gerber, a surgeon in Los Angeles, testified as follows concerning unnecessary surgery.

DR. GERBER: In my particular field of surgery at the present time there are many unnecessary and ineptly performed operations by unqualified and untrained men. And these lead our statistics to go askew. Right here in California the medically indigent children under the Medi-Cal plan have their tonsils removed ten times more frequently than the other children in the private sector of medicine. . . .

SENATOR KENNEDY: Do we have too many tonsillectomies? . . .

DR. GERBER: Yes; because I think Swedish children are just as healthy as American children and the incidence of tonsillectomies in Sweden is one tenth as high as it is in California. . . .

SENATOR KENNEDY: Why do you think there are that number of surgical operations?

DR. GERBER: Because we have a double standard of medical care in this country. Because we have one group of patients who get the very best that the world has to offer and another group of patients who get probably some of the worst. And the reason is that we do not control the practice of medicine strictly enough in our hospitals. We find that doctors who would be barred from operating at the Veterans' Hospital or at a well-regulated civilian hospital can operate with impunity at some of the smaller unregulated hospitals in this country. That is why I say we have a double standard. To make it worse, you can't tell the player by his number. It is perfectly possible for a doctor who has not had a single day of surgical training in his life beyond his internship to list his name in the yellow pages of the directory as a surgeon, or in any other specialty, for that matter. There is no law that says that a doctor can't call himself a pediatrician or a gynecologist or what-have-you, just by self-proclamation.

Perhaps the reason so much surgery is done is the fact that there are so many surgeons and that surgery pays so well. According to the American Medical Association, surgeons in 1968 had the second-highest incomes of all the medical specialties. Even including residents and interns, their average incomes were over $40,000 per year. Many make several times that figure. The attraction of high income may also account for the fact that of the 278,000 physicians practicing medicine in 1970, some 28,000, or over ten percent, were general surgeons and 82,000, or almost thirty percent, were in one or another of the surgical specialties.

Other fields than surgery have been implicated as providing unnecessary services. Dr. Lowell E. Bellin, first deputy commissioner of the New York City Health Department, testified concerning a study his department did of the quality of dental care given patients whose bills were paid under Medicaid in New York City. He said:

We called in about thirteen hundred patients who had received dental services, in an attempt to assess the quality of dental work that they had received. There I would point out that it is technically feasible to assess quality of dental care. Anyone in this room, for example, if examined by any one of the forty-two dentists on my payroll, will soon learn, within ten or fifteen minutes, what is the quality of the dentures, what is the quality of the fillings, that he has received during the last four or five years. And we found as we called in these thirteen hundred people that nine percent of the patients had received quality of care that would have resulted in the immediate flunking out of any dental student who would have tried to perpetuate this quality of work. Another nine percent we could not ascertain the care at all in the mouth because simple fraud had been carried out—we had been billed for work that in fact had not taken place.

And in dollars-and-cents values, something like twenty-five percent of the dentures that we found in another study we found to represent overutilization—that is, services performed without either therapeutical or preventive justification. So that we had this troika of abuse: We had (1) poor quality, (2) fraud, and (3) overutilization. . . .

And I want to quickly say this: The total number of professionals who are carrying on such abuse is a very small number. The majority of professionals are decent, excellent, prudent men who are trying to do a good job. Our working statistic based upon four and a half years experience in this town is that about five to ten percent of the practitioners represent abusers.

INADEQUATE SERVICES

In addition to poor-quality care and unnecessary services, many Americans simply receive incomplete health care services.

We have already seen in earlier chapters evidence of the heavy work loads and long waiting lines in public hospitals and have heard cases of hurried and mistaken diagnoses and treatment.

We have also seen how fragmentation of the system into numerous specialists practicing in relative isolation from each other can result in differing or late diagnoses and a poorer quality of care.

We have heard how shortages of physicians in rural and inner-city areas result in omitting basic preventive care such as immunizations, Pap smears, and chest X rays as well as follow-up care. Dr. Weil indicated that, based on the shortage of physicians alone, two thirds of the children in the country are getting anywhere from no care at all to inadequate or minimal care.

We have also seen how pressures of work load and financial needs lead providers to delay care, turn patients aside, or treat them in a peremptory manner.

Problems of this sort impact on all Americans. They affect the middle-income Americans as well as the poor and the rich. These problems are there because of the short supply of physicians and other health professionals and the archaic way professionals are organized to deliver health care. As is frequently the case, however, these problems impact most heavily on low-income families. Those who have limited funds have contact with the busiest and least responsive part of the health care system. They have no choice but to go to the doctor, dentist, or hospital where they will be given care free or at reduced costs. In such situations, the lines are frequently longer and treatment more hurried, and more health problems are simply left untended. The overall quality of care is certainly lower for Americans in such situations than for Americans who can pay and do at least have a fighting chance at all the necessary health services.

For the Reverend Tom Chapman, pastor of the Avon Baptist Church in Cleveland, Ohio, the problem was not so much being poor as it was being suspected of being poor because he is black. As Mr. Chapman put it in describing the lack of attention given his wife one night in a hospital emergency room:

. . . where people become geared or colored by attitudes that say they don't give a damn about people or don't really care, it doesn't matter if a person has money or doesn't have money, because these kinds of patterns have set in, and they become a part of that person's makeup. And this was the kind of thing I think was happening that night. We had Blue Cross and I had presented a Blue Cross card.

Mr. Chapman's treatment, however, may be more typical of treatment of the poor than we dare imagine. He told the following story.

MR. CHAPMAN: It was in 1968, in August, about ten-thirty, eleven at night that my wife, Marie, fell in our home. We helped her to the bed and discovered that the pain was so intense at that time that she would need medical attention. So we called the emergency crew, and they came out and they did take her to St. Luke's Hospital. We arrived there, I guess, about eleven-thirty.

About twelve or twelve-thirty, she got to see a doctor there, who immediately sent her to get some X rays in the area of her back where she said she was hurting. They returned about, oh, twenty minutes later and the doctor told me she was okay, that I could take her home. I went in to assist her, but she insisted that she couldn't move. And at this I went back to the doctor and I related to him that Marie says that she can't move, the pain was that intense. So he went back into the room, and of course I stepped out, and when I went back again after he had left the room again where he was waiting on her, she was crying, of course, and she says, "Chapman, the doctor wants me to go back home, but I can't hardly move, the pain is too much."

So I go back again and talk to the doctor and he says, "Well, listen, your wife has had a fall, she's got a pinched nerve in her back and she is in pain and that is to be expected. Now I am the doctor and she is okay, so take her home."

And I said, "Well, I know my wife. We have been married fifteen years now, and I know she is not a pretender, she can take pain, she has been ill before." So I refused to take her home. I went out to the waiting room.

He and a nurse went back, and it was about fifteen minutes later that they were back there with her and they brought her out in a wheelchair, and what they had done was to dress her and basically lift her from the place she was lying, dressed her, sat her in a wheelchair, and brought her out to me, and they said, "Now take her home."

Well, at this point I don't believe that is the thing to do. So I told the doctor I am not going to take her home, because I believe she ought to be kept here and further attention or examination ought to be given.

He says, "It's your wife, you do what you want to do, I am through." So he goes back to the office, and I sat there and my wife sat there in a wheelchair. It was about, oh, two in the morning now, and of course by this time all the other emergency traffic had been cleared away, and we were the only ones there.

The doctor goes back into another little room, I guess that is where he sleeps, and about three-thirty he came out again and he saw that we were still there. He went back into the little room. And he came back in about another hour and we were still there.

So it was about four-thirty, five that my wife wanted to go to the bathroom. And of course she couldn't get any help here, because they had discharged her and I couldn't take her into the ladies' rest room nor the men's rest room. So she sat there until around seven, six maybe.

I called the Academy of Medicine. It being Saturday morning, they were closed and I didn't get any answer. Of course, I did reach their answering service, which is all a taped system.

Well, at this time I encourage my wife just to release herself there. Her bladder was full, and I said, "Well, just go right where you are." Well, she couldn't do that. Of course, by this time I had no alternative but to try to get her to the bathroom, at least to the door. And as she did get to the door and finally into the bathroom and back to the chair again, I concluded that since she had been that mobile on her own account, that possibly I could take her home and do as the doctor had prescribed, which was to take sitz baths twice a day.

So finally I literally picked her up and carried her to the car. We drove home, and I literally carried her into the house, put her in bed, and began her first sitz-bath operation. And that kept on for the next few days, and the pain did not subside.

So eventually we concluded that there had to be something wrong which X rays maybe did not reveal. So we carried her then to the Lakeside Hospital, where she in fact was given extensive X rays. And they did discover that there were several vertebrae broken in her back. And for weeks she had been laboring, going through those processes of sitz baths and up and down. And of course at this point I just felt that there was something that ought to be done. And I sought legal advice as to what we should do to find satisfaction for the kind of damage that I felt as a result of this terrible situation.

SENATOR KENNEDY: You mean that all the time they were prescribing remedies for a pinched nerve, she had these fractured or dislocated or broken vertebrae?

MR. CHAPMAN: Broken vertebrae.

SENATOR KENNEDY: Their examination had failed to reveal that?

MR. CHAPMAN: There was only one X ray, as I understand, that was given, which was not quite as extensive as I think should have been at this time. I think there was neglect on the part of the hospital to really perform the kind of research or examination to discover this.

AMERICANS CAN'T TELL IF THEY ARE GETTING QUALITY CARE

The examples, claims, and statistics discussed above do not show that all American medical care is poor. Much of it is the best. They do show, however, that it varies in quality. The fact is that quality of care varies greatly. Even more troublesome, we are not in a position to know whether we are getting good care or not—nor do the health care professionals and institutions do enough to guarantee the quality of the health care we receive.

Sanford Kravitz, Ph.D., dean of the School of Social Welfare at the State University of New York at Stony Brook, participated in an extensive inquiry into health services for Americans. He testified in New York as follows.

DR. KRAVITZ: I consider myself a relatively sophisticated person in this area, and I know that I have no adequate way of judging for myself the quality of care which I get. I happen to be in the fortunate position of being in an institution which has a large number of well-qualified physicians, so I can, as a friend and colleague, call for responsible judgments. I am at a loss to know how someone who is not in that fortunate position knows whether or not they are getting quality care. And I am talking about the middle-class, upper-middle-class, higher-income person, who has the capacity to go out and purchase the care, has a car to drive, is physically able to do so. . . .

The middle- or upper-income person has no reason to expect that they would get any better quality care in dealing with an individual practitioner or an institution than a poor person. The chances are they might. They just might, because they have somewhat more choice available to them. But they have no guarantees that this system will provide them with quality care.

SENATOR KENNEDY: Do you think they really understand that?

DR. KRAVITZ: No, I don't think that they understand that, Senator.

Unfortunately, few of us are able to judge where to get the best health care; we simply don't know enough to make that decision. We may choose a doctor, a dentist, a nursing home, or other providers of health care for many reasons. They may be convenient to our home. They may be efficient and have short waiting lines. They may have attractive facilities. They may have a reassuring and friendly manner. They may seem thorough and may discuss our problems thoroughly with us. We are in a position to judge all these things and choose on the basis of them. However, we don't know how to tell if the provider is up to date with the latest literature, respected by other physicians as being the best, good, or only fair, or generally whether he is capable enough to give us the care we want. The fact is that the quality of care varies, and we do not know which providers are offering the best care and which are offering the worst.

In fact, the health care system operates in ways which keep us from information that might enable us to choose the best care:

Physicians hesitate or refuse outright to comment on care given by a patient's previous or other physicians, as a matter of professional ethics. Thus we find it hard to get another professional opinion of a doctor's work, unless we happen to be personal friends with a doctor and in a position to get his confidential advice on who the best physicians are in an area.

Physicians send us to the hospital where they have staff privileges, not necessarily to the hospital we might choose. We realize only at the time we are hospitalized that in choosing a physician we also chose a hospital.

There is no *Consumer Reports* in health care. No agency has undertaken to describe and rate by quality and cost the care offered by various providers.

Health care institutions do not advertise to inform us of their advantages.

Insurance companies, even non-profit corporations such as Blue Cross and Blue Shield, do not make public their criteria for reviewing bills for the reasonableness of the care offered and its cost, nor do they make public those individuals or institutions who offer questionable services.

Some of these restrictions on the American's right to know and choose wisely are overdone. Dr. Kravitz insisted:

The witness from Blue Shield testified on the kind of criteria which they internally use within that system. Well, people outside the system ought to know this. Consumers ought to know what represents an overexpenditure of funds, misuse of time, too many drugs being given, and so forth. I am sure that information is not generally shared with the public about those people who do misuse these programs. We ought to make public those institutions, those individuals who misuse these programs in this way so that they can be held up for public condemnation and can be avoided by the consumer.

The professions protect themselves, and all professions— my own included—that operate in the system maintaining waste "do not rock the boat." And until we begin to educate the public as to what are reasonable and responsible expectations that we can demand of professionals and institutions, the public will not know what is good quality care.

### SOLO PRACTICE HAMPERS QUALITY CARE

But the public does not and cannot bear the total burden of choosing quality care and avoiding poor quality. The professions owe themselves and the public maximum effort to guarantee the quality of care. By establishing education and licensure requirements for doctors, dentists, nurses, hospitals, medical schools, and many others, the providers have in fact greatly improved the quality of care. However, there is much more to be done.

Dr. Michael De Bakey, the famed heart surgeon, testified:

I think we have a better system in medical research for, say, controlling the quality of research, because it is on a competitive basis. There is a built-in mechanism by which the scientific community itself, through peers, evaluates continually the program, and we simply don't have anything like this in the delivery of health care.

Some efforts are being made by professionals to guarantee a higher quality of care. We have heard from Blue Cross/ Blue Shield of computer screening of insurance claims, using various criteria of quality of care and reasonableness of cost. Through such techniques the insurer hopes to detect fraud, excessive services and unreasonable charges. These techniques have in fact resulted in significant savings to the insurance company by enabling the company to refuse to pay such claims, to pay them in lower amounts, or even to expel offending providers from participation in the plan.

In another area, Dr. Lawrence Weed of the University of Vermont described the utility of new types of standard medical records that allow physicians to keep better track of a patient's history and, more importantly, allow one physician to benefit from and make a critique of the health care offered by another physician. Dr. F. Morgan Pruyn testified in Mt. Kisco, New York, to the utility of such records, especially when kept by physicians in group practice. Dr. Pruyn emphasized the review that physicians in his group make of one another's work during the routine course of business.

All of these efforts, however, have major shortcomings. The insurance company's review is based on charges and other data on the insurance claim. The majority of health services offered are not covered by insurance, and of that which is covered only a small percentage can adequately be reviewed for quality on the basis of the insurance claim. This system might find unnecessary charges or overcharges, but it would not, for example, identify a patient whose surgery was unnecessary because the diagnosis was in error. It is better at identifying fraud or abuse than inadequate training, negligence or incompetence for the particular service rendered.

While new medical records are hopeful improvements, unless they are diligently kept and are reviewed by other physicians they are of minimal value.

Of the 192,000 practicing physicians in America who practice from their offices, over 152,000 are in solo practice. A physician in such a situation is less likely to keep thorough records, according to Dr. Pruyn, because the records are only for his own use and it is easy to put them off until tomorrow. Moreover, the records of physicians in solo practice are seldom reviewed by other physicians. Most physicians encounter review only when they admit a patient to a hospital, and even then the extent of the review varies widely depending on the hospital, the nature of the case, and other factors. The fact is that the vast majority of health care offered in this country by physicians, dentists, and other health professionals is never reviewed by other health professionals. Moreover, nowhere in all our hearings did we hear of effective ways to guarantee the quality of care offered in solo practice.

In addition to contributing to the fragmentation of care, the solo practice of medicine seems to be a fundamental roadblock to the health profession's guaranteeing the quality of care. The profession can offer no guarantees of the quality of its members' work if it sees little or no evidence of this day-to-day work. Dr. Pruyn's testimony was very clear in distinguishing between peer review in groups as opposed to solo practice.

SENATOR KENNEDY: What can you do to assure quality control?

DR. PRUYN: I think it is the built-in peer review. The record of a patient is the property, you might say, of the medical group, and if I were not to be in the office today and one of my patients came in, that patient's records would be reviewed by the physician who was going to look after the patient. If it wasn't considered a good record, I would be called on the carpet about it. The very fact that I know my work is going to be reviewed is an incentive to the lazy doctor who might ordinarily cut the corner.

And I think these are all the advantages of working in unison with people. It has a profound influence on the quality of care, and also on the urge to try and keep up with the young fellows that are coming along after you.

SENATOR KENNEDY: Of course, that wouldn't exist in terms of solo practice, would it?

DR. PRUYN: No.

SENATOR KENNEDY: And there really is very little peer review done for solo practice across the country as I understand.

DR. PRUYN: Well, it is hard to see how it could be done. Private records are not reviewable by any person who wanted to do such a thing. You could subpoena them, I suppose, but you certainly couldn't walk in the doctor's office and review records, because they are privileged communication. Patients would raise the roof.

SENATOR KENNEDY: Well, how do you meet the problems of quality? How can people know when they go to a doctor in a given community and he prescribes *x*, that *x* is really the best in terms of their problem? They can't shop around and look for someone else. They have confidence in this doctor, but do they have to just take it on faith? . . .

DR. PRUYN: Well, this would mean showing records, which you don't usually do. You see, if you keep records only for yourself you can be pretty sketchy and you can say you will do it tomorrow. If you have partners who may need the record tomorrow, you can't put it off, and I think this is what I said. Certainly in a hospital they make tremendous efforts to keep the records good. I don't think you can do that in solo practice.

In all our hearings and in all our conferences with professionals in the health care field, we saw no way for the health system to guarantee quality of care without major changes in the way health professionals organize themselves. In the current solo-practice–dominated system, efforts to improve quality require clumsy compromises that are more concerned with maintaining the providers' existing style of life than with assuring quality care to the people. Even at best they often offer fast and sporadic reviews of diagnoses and treatment, rather than ongoing interchanges among physicians during diagnosis and treatment in an environment which encourages continuing education and professional growth.

## MY CONVICTION

*Fundamental changes need to be made both in what the public is told about health services and in the amount of responsibility that professionals accept for guaranteeing the quality of care.*

*At the very least, the public should have access to information on the extreme cases of providers who abuse the patient by overcharging, by performing unnecessary work, or by simply not providing an acceptable quality of care. If a patient feels he has been treated poorly, he should have enough information to allow him to choose another provider on an informed basis.*

*In any other industry, if someone felt he was offering a better product or a less expensive product, he would tell the public about it. In health care, if a group of doctors practicing together review one another's work, allow time off for further education, and otherwise assure higher-quality care, they should tell the public about it. This would provide a competition among physicians that would encourage changes in other physicians' practices, and at the same time give the public the information it needs in order to make the most informed choice possible.*

*Perhaps more fundamentally, however, we should require the health care professions to assume a greater responsibility for guaranteeing the quality of care. It is intolerable that many providers place less emphasis on the quality of care for the patient than on their own preferred style of life. This will require changes in the training of health professionals and shifts in economic and other incentives to assure a realistic distribution of physicians by specialty. It will require efforts to improve the distribution of professionals geographically. But most of all it will require changes in the way physicians organize to provide health care.*

*This may mean that many physicians will have to give up their solo or single-specialty-group practices. Possibly new computer and communications equipment, as well as new forms of peer review, will enable some physicians to remain in solo practice, especially in areas of the country where other modes of practice prove impractical. Even so, solo practice should have to prove its quality in competition with other modes of practice.*

*I believe that a system of national health insurance will encourage such changes.*

CHAPTER VII

# Businessmen or Healers?

"DEAR Sir: Unless payment in full in the amount of $2,597.62 reaches this office by May 23rd, 1969, or satisfactory arrangements to settle this account are made, your case will be processed for legal action without further notice to you."

A hospital sent this letter on May 13, 1969, to Mr. Fernando Chavez, whose income is ninety dollars a week. Many, Americans receive such letters from hospitals or physicians, sometimes after struggling to pay off a debt in small installments. Sometimes the letter is from the hospital or the doctor, and sometimes it is from a professional collection agency—such as in the following story of Mrs. Smythe.

SENATOR KENNEDY: And you have been paying St. Luke's $150 a month on their bill?
MRS. SMYTHE: Ever since he [Mr. Smythe] got out, yes.
SENATOR KENNEDY: How long has that been?
MRS. SMYTHE: Well, a year and a half. And of course,

177

St. Luke's knows this man can't go to work, so I don't know how they expect it to be paid. They have turned it over to a collection agency, because they don't have time to bother with you.

SENATOR KENNEDY: A collection agency. They are one of the fastest-growing health businesses in the country. What happened when your husband tried to get back into St. Luke's?

MRS. SMYTHE: When he went in for the surgery on the incision, they immediately put him in a room, and they sent word for me to come right down to the office and pay them before the surgery could be done, because we had no credit.

SENATOR KENNEDY: Even though you had been paying off at $150 a month?

MRS. SMYTHE: This doesn't make any difference.

SENATOR KENNEDY: And they were aware of your income?

MRS. SMYTHE: Yes.

SENATOR KENNEDY: And they still required that you put up a deposit before they would go ahead with surgery?

MRS. SMYTHE: That's right, and when he went back in last September for the heart catheterization, once again there had to be cash beforehand.

SENATOR KENNEDY: Could you have gone to another hospital?

MRS. SMYTHE: No.

SENATOR KENNEDY: Why not?

MRS. SMYTHE: Because our surgeon operates only at St. Luke's. . . . My husband could have gone to the Veterans' Hospital. He is a veteran. But here, once again, the doctor couldn't go there to operate.

SENATOR KENNEDY: Are you happy with the doctor?

MRS. SMYTHE: Oh, I think he's the most marvelous man

I ever saw, and I'm not saying that he's expensive, because the bill was not large for what he did.

These stories reveal a side of our health care system that more and more Americans see. They reveal the "business" side of health care, the concern with income or profit. There are similar examples throughout this book and in the experience of every family—reminders that those whom Americans respect deeply as "healers" are also in some sense businessmen very conscious of income or profit, entrepreneurs who cherish their right to do business wherever, however, and at whatever prices the market will support.

### HEALTH CARE PROVIDERS ARE INCOME-CONSCIOUS

We have heard dozens of stories of income-conscious hospitals, physicians, dentists and other providers.

We've heard stories of people who are turned away by hospitals unless they can make deposits or can show evidence of insurance; people ejected from a dentist's office or their hospital rooms because their insurance was inadequate or had run out; people who are told, quite falsely, that they cannot leave the hospital until their bill is paid; people who are hounded by collection agencies that buy the hospitals' and doctors' "bad debts" or get a percentage of what they collect; people who are forced into bankruptcy by their medical bills and forced afterwards to pay *before* they are treated; people who must resort to overcrowded, inadequate public-hospital emergency rooms because, for economic reasons, private hospitals have closed their emergency rooms and private physicians have moved away.

Not all providers of health care are equally income-conscious, nor do they have the same reasons for this consciousness. For the physician in private practice, it is a matter of personal income level. For proprietary hospitals, it is a matter of showing a profit for the owners or stockholders. For the nonprofit hospitals, it is a matter of balancing the budget —of meeting the salaries and paying the bills. Regardless of the reason, most health care providers are very income-conscious today.

Physicians, dentists, and other health professionals vary greatly in how income-conscious they are. I have talked with physicians who in fact give large amounts of time to serving those who cannot pay at all and who are quick to adjust their charges to those for whom the regular charge would be a terrible hardship. At the other extreme, there are physicians who make sure they treat only people who can pay their full price. Many physicians in between these extremes locate their practice, establish their fees, and use collection agencies and billing techniques as necessary to assure a good income. Physicians' charges rose sixty percent from 1960 to 1970. Even back in 1968 the average physician's income in America was over $35,000 per year—an average that includes interns and residents, who generally made less than one quarter of this amount. Even in 1968, many, many physicians made a great deal more than $35,000. In 1969, the average physician worked fifty-one hours a week for his income.

Nonprofit private hospitals also vary in how income-conscious they are. Many in fact managed to keep their budgets balanced and offer services to anyone who comes to their door without closing emergency rooms or resorting to tough collection procedures. After failing to find a single private hospital with an open emergency room in Queens County, New York, I was pleased to see in Cleveland that nearly every hospital operated such a facility. Even in Cleveland, however, the handwriting was on the wall. Several private hospitals had already announced that they would have to cut back their outpatient and emergency-room activities unless they could obtain more funds.

Many private nonprofit hospitals are so pressed for funds that they are forced to be extremely income-conscious. Mr. James Campbell, president of the Rush–Presbyterian–St. Luke's Medical Center in Chicago told us, "As purveyors, we are victims because our people depend upon us for their bread and butter." Indeed, in recent years the cost to hospitals for wages and for specialized equipment and facilities has risen rapidly, forcing rises in room rates, tougher efforts to collect bills, and, in some hospitals, efforts to screen patients and reduce the number admitted who cannot pay. Such stringent measures may seem inconsistent with the nonprofit, tax-exempt nature of these institutions. The fact that they resort to such measures is an indication of the great financial pressures under which they operate. To meet these pressures, hospital charges rose 170 percent from 1960 to 1970.

Moreover, 858 hospitals in America, with 59,000 beds, are owned and operated for profit. For these hospitals, it is not just a matter of being income-conscious, it is a matter of being profit-conscious. Their practices vary widely according to the degree of profit-consciousness among their owners.

We cannot blame providers for trying to make a good income, balance their budgets, or make a good profit for their stockholders. But we must ask, Does the provider's income-consciousness have to result in the people's paying higher costs, getting less care, or being subject to harassment and bankruptcy? Is their income-consciousness a constructive or a destructive thing?

### HEALTH CARE PROVIDERS AS ENTREPRENEURS

There is a spirit among hospitals, physicians, dentists, and other providers that they can set up business with whatever fees the market will allow. Each provider is a business to himself in this sense. This is not unlike other businesses, whose owners set up wherever they choose and do business in whatever way they choose, the only limitation being whether or not people will buy their product.

Physicians and hospitals seem to cherish this freedom. The large majority of physicians choose to set up solo practices or single-specialty group practices in suburban communities in America. We have also seen hospitals exercise the same option of moving to suburban communities. Others limit their admissions to patients referred by private physicians and close down their walk-in outpatient clinics and emergency rooms. These practices help assure that the hospital's clientele will be able to pay their bills.

Hospitals also express this entrepreneurial spirit by competing with one another for prestige within the professional community to attract top-notch staff. This may mean adding sophisticated new equipment. Dr. Lloyd Elam of Meharry Medical College pointed out that in order to attract top physicians to their staffs hospitals frequently buy equipment that would otherwise be unnecessary.

We cannot blame the hospitals or the physicians for exercising this free-entrepreneurial spirit. However, we must ask the question, Does this spirit lead providers to find ways to deliver higher-quality, less fragmented and more accessible care to the people? Does this spirit have to result in more and more physicians going into suburban areas to practice, leaving Americans in rural and inner-city areas with less and less accessible health care; in more and more physicians choosing to enter specialties and further fragmenting health services; in most physicians choosing to remain in solo practice even though it is harder to guarantee quality care in such practices; and, finally, in the price of health care getting higher and higher and a bigger obstacle to more and more Americans?

### THE HEALTH CARE INDUSTRY IS BAD BUSINESS

There is nothing wrong with being a business. In fact, the businessman's concern with income and profit, and the entrepreneurial spirit that sets up business wherever and however will prove profitable are creative forces in our society. As businesses compete to attract people as customers, they produce better or higher-quality products or services for the people. By and large, despite abuses of these ideas, Americans believe that the man who profits most in his business is the man who gives the people what they want and need. It's the old story of "build a better mousetrap and the world will beat a path to your door." We also believe that if a businessman makes an inferior product or offers a poor service he will not stay in business for very long. In a nutshell, good business and profits go together with giving good service to the people.

Unfortunately, this simply does not hold true of health care. Income-consciousness and the entrepreneurial spirit lead health care providers to offer most Americans fragmented care and little assurance of quality, and to leave many Americans with inadequate care or no care at all. Unlike other industries, there is no competition among providers of health care, there is a seemingly unlimited market for services, there are monopolistic practices, and, finally and most importantly, the American people cannot judge the quality or relative cost of the services they are offered.

In fact, it hardly makes sense—despite the insistence of organized medicine—to look at health care as a business or free enterprise in the American sense at all. Lacking the basic elements of competition and free choice by the consumer, it is, at best, *bad business.*

Unlike other businesses, physicians and hospitals do not compete with each other for the people's business. In a given city, hospitals' room rates and reputations for quality vary markedly. In New York, for example, daily rates vary from under $75 to almost $150. The average patient, even with insurance, pays a percentage of this cost directly, over and above the cost of his insurance premiums. Yet the average patient usually learns the hospitals' charges only when he is released, and he is given little or no choice about which hospital he goes to. He will be referred to a hospital where his physician is on the staff and where his physician finds it convenient to place him. The patient has no opportunity to shop or to compare either rates or reputations for quality. Nor do the hospitals and doctors encourage such shopping by advertising or publishing their rates.

Likewise, there is little or no competition among physicians. It would be difficult to get an estimate from several physicians on a particular surgical or other procedure. Shopping of this type is frowned upon by most physicians.

### LACK OF COMPETITION ON QUALITY

Nor can Americans compare their physicians on the basis of the quality of care they offer. As pointed out in an earlier chapter, Americans may choose their physician on the basis

of his convenience, his personality, or his seeming thorough-
ness, but they can't really judge the quality of care he offers.
In fact, the study cited in Chapter VI indicates that even
among those who received care of questionable quality most
of the patients felt they received good care and were well
pleased. The fact is that the patient can't know the quality
of physician care he is getting, nor is another physician likely
to tell him if he can offer higher-quality care. In all our hearings, it is difficult to get physicians even to state publicly that
some physicians are more qualified than others.

### MONOPOLISTIC PRACTICES

Indeed, far from competing, the activities of some medical
organizations look like monopolistic practices. In twenty-two
states in this country there are laws, usually heavily supported
by the medical societies, which restrict the formation of prepaid group practices—a type of medical organization that
claims to offer more health services for less money than the
current solo-practice fee-for-service systems. When we were
in Iowa, the state medical society was involved in a fight to
keep a law on the books which prevented physicians from
practicing medicine on a salaried basis; they wanted time to
set up another form of practice more to their liking before
being faced with the competition of this new form of practice.
Such laws in the twenty-two states assure control by the
states' medical societies of how medicine is practiced, and
help to stifle competition.

Medical-society resistance to group practice is not limited
to legal maneuvers in twenty-two states, however. Doctors in
every prepaid group practice that we have visited describe
how in their early years they were ostracized by other physi-

cians and in some cases were actually denied admission to the medical societies. Many of the groups are still so worried about the opinions of their peers that they do not wish to publicly describe their early experiences with other physicians. Indeed, medical societies and the American Medical Association seem often more concerned with defending an entrenched, competition-free position for their members than with promoting competition and innovation to find new ways of filling health care needs of Americans.

A physician can make a good income wherever and however he practices. Thus he is under little financial pressure to go where the need is greatest, offer his services in a less fragmented way, make efforts to guarantee the quality of his service, keep his prices down, or do any of the other things businessmen usually do to compete for customers. Patients end up buying his services wherever and however he sells them. This is the essence of a "seller's market." All the advantages are with the man selling health care and none with the man buying it, because the latter has little or no real choice.

There is some indication, moreover, that this seller's market does not result only because there are not enough doctors, and that people *need* more health services so badly that they buy anything they can get. In fact, indications are that many people get more surgery, more dental care, and more services in general than they actually need. The problem may be in part that Americans aren't in a position to tell whether they actually need the services or whether the services are a luxury or even inadvisable. If the physician needs the business, he may not tell them.

## THE PEOPLE HAVE NO SAY

The result of the lack of competition, the monopolistic practices, the seller's market, and the people's inability to judge quality is that the providers do not have to respond to what the people want. To put it another way, because health care is "bad business" the people have little say or influence over the cost of care, the quality of care, or how it is offered. The people can, of course, choose their physician and they should always have that right, but because there is no competition among physicians, no incentive to offer new and more attractive services, the people don't really have many options. The people can't tell the physicians apart; all of the physicians seem to be offering about the same thing.

The American people do have a say in most businesses in this country. For example, if enough people express interest in small cars, the auto industries will start making them. In fact, if an auto manufacturer senses a new trend in what the people want, he will try to market a product to meet this interest before his competition, or at a better price, or at a higher quality. The people do have a say on what kinds of automobiles are sold—and on their cost.

The big difference, of course, is that the people have a wider choice in other businesses; they are in a better position to make an informed choice; and they profit from vigorous competition among the providers. But there is little competition among health care providers. I am convinced that income consciousness and the entrepreneurial spirit among providers in the absence of true competition and consumer choice will never contribute to solving the problems in our health care system. For example, physicians and hospitals will always charge pretty much what they choose to charge. They can be confident there will be little or no shopping around by the patients. Because the people have no choice, they are able to put very little pressure on the hospitals and doctors to keep costs down. Because there is no competition, the physicians and hospitals feel no strong pressure from one another.

The tragic thing is that there are less costly ways to provide health care. Statistics on the prepaid-group-practice plans, for example, show much lower hospital costs and lower office-visit costs on a per-patient basis. Yet such organizations offer broader health services than most Americans currently have available. Unfortunately, the people do not have this option offered to them by the health care providers. This type of organization requires physicians to work on salaries or under other arrangements which are distasteful to many physicians. Providers do not start such organizations because they feel no pressure to respond to a possible market the way the auto or retail industry does, or to hold down their costs to remain competitive. There is no competition.

Similarly, hospitals feel no strong pressure toward efficiency or toward economizing on special-equipment costs by forming sharing agreements with other hospitals. In many cities there are more specialty units—such as open-heart surgical units—than can be efficiently used. Their cost is added to everyone's hospital bill, regardless of the nature of your illness. Many hospitals, in fact, are far more interested in competing for prestige in the medical community than in competing for patients by keeping down costs. Lacking pressures from the people and competition within the industry, health care prices are rising much faster than the rest of our economy.

These same factors also contribute heavily to the fragmentation of health services, the varying quality of health services, the oversupply of some specialists and undersupply of others, the uneven distribution of physicians across the country, and other problems in our health care system. Lacking competition or pressure from the people, what is the incentive to providers for finding better ways to organize care to decrease fragmentation and increase quality—especially if such organization means that the provider must give up some of the independence he cherishes? If a physician can always make a good living, why not go into the specialty or the geographic area he finds most lucrative or interesting? What is the incentive to go into specialties or areas where the people need him most?

We do not know what kinds of new health care organizations might be developed if health care providers felt the same creative incentives the rest of American businesses feel. I am convinced that the doctors, dentists, hospital administrators and others can and would create better health care systems for all Americans if these incentives existed to channel the income-consciousness and the enterpreneurial spirit into efforts responsive to the American people's need. I am also convinced that without such incentives, physicians and other providers will increasingly lose the respect they so richly deserve as healers and earn in its place disrespect as businessmen taking advantage of an unfair market.

## MY CONVICTION

*America should take actions to assure the rights and freedoms of those who need care while assuring the rights of the providers of health care. We must guarantee the doctor's right to be both businessman* and *healer by taking actions which make sure that it is good business to respond to the needs and demands of the people for healing.*

I do not believe *we should take away the physician's right to do business.* I do not believe *we should "socialize" medicine, making doctors and all other health professionals employees on salary from the government.*

*I* do *believe we must find ways to give the people a choice, and an opportunity to influence the cost, quality, and organization of health care. I believe the government must intervene in the health care industry to make it a fairer market than it is.*

*America should take action to eliminate monopolistic practices in medicine; encourage providers to form new and competitive types of health care systems; and allow the people to choose among types of health care on the basis of cost, comprehensiveness of services, the manner of their organization, and personal preferences.*

*America should assure its doctors, dentists, and other health professionals the right to choose their style of practice, their specialty, and the location of their practice, while at the same time offering incentives comparable to those felt in other businesses to pratice in a manner, in a specialty, and in a place where the people's need is the greatest.*

*Given competition and other incentives to control costs and improve services, America must assure that every American can pay for needed health care. If physicians and hospitals alike can collect a reasonable fee for health services rendered to any American, they can give every attention to healing and not turn people away or resort to harsh collection methods.*

CHAPTER VIII

# The Health Insurance Trap

IN 1970, over ninety-four percent of Americans under age
sixty-five, more than 170 million people, had some form of
private health insurance. (Most Americans over sixty-five,
of course, have Medicare.) The insurance industry in this
same year paid out $17 billion in benefits to Americans. Of
this, almost $8 billion was paid out by nonprofit organiza-
tions, such as Blue Cross/Blue Shield, and over $9 billion
by private, profit-making insurance companies. There are
over 1,800 organizations in the United States that sell health
insurance.

In the last twenty years, health insurance coverages have
expanded greatly, and more and more Americans have come
under insurance plans—through their unions, through their
employers, or through purchase of individual policies.

The large and growing private health insurance industry
would seem at first glance to be a way to reduce the high cost
of health care and to improve the quality and organization
of our health care. Private insurance is, after all, a way for
Americans to pool their assets and share the risks of illness,

as I recommended in Chapter II. Through insurance, we all pay regular premiums while we are healthy, and we collect from the pool for our costs if we get sick. The insurance mechanism has in fact already eased the impact of health care costs on millions of Americans. Some people argue that with some improvements it could cover the families stricken with catastrophic expenses such as those described in Chapter I. Indeed, if insurance allowed all Americans to share the risks equally, the costs of premiums might even be low enough that low-income families could buy insurance.

Moreover, it might seem that as millions of Americans enroll in insurance plans, the insurance agencies might serve as the people's representatives with hospitals, physicians, and other providers. While individual Americans may not be able by their choices to control costs and encourage better organization and higher-quality care, surely an insurer representing thousands or even millions of Americans could have an influence. The insurance organization would seem to be a way for people to have a say in health care.

Some of the health insurance industry, and many others, believe that the health insurance industry can in fact perform these functions for America. I do not believe they can. Looking at their record to date, listening to stories of people whose insurance let them down, and hearing testimony on the industry's unsuccessful recent efforts, I feel they will never be able to fill these functions.

### HEALTH INSURANCE: ITS TRAPS AND SURPRISES

Health insurance coverages are so complex that they bewilder most Americans. Most of us do not know what our policy pays for until we receive the hospital or doctor bill, and then we are frequently surprised at how much of it we must pay ourselves. Unfortunately, many Americans discover when the bill comes that they have no coverage at all, while other Americans with low incomes have given up on being able to afford health insurance.

## *People Whose Coverage Is Inadequate*

We have already seen in earlier chapters story after story of Americans who thought they were better protected than they really were. There was Mr. Leonard Kunken, who felt that a $40,000 maximum limit would cover any of his needs, until his son's football accident ran up $50,000 in five months, with no end in sight. There was Mrs. De Witt, who felt that her policy would cover her delivery and her newborn infant, only to find that the fixed amount paid in maternity benefits was not nearly enough to cover current hospital and doctor prices, and that she had to pay for her infant's $6,000 operation because her policy didn't cover newborn infants during their first fifteen days of life. There was Mr. Ralph Tresky, who found out that his policy did not cover doctor fees for his wife's kidney dialysis in the hospital or the thousands of dollars in costs of dialysis at home.

There are many, many others. Nearly every story in this book involves an American whose insurance ran out, excluded certain services or diseases, or required deductibles and partial payments by the policyholder which ran up to thousands of dollars before they were through. In some cases the family was bankrupted, in others long-accumulated savings were wiped out, and in many others debts were incurred which required regular payments that mortgaged a family's future.

It is not surprising to me that Americans do not know what their insurance covers until they see the bill. There are so many insurance policies, with so many different payment schedules, deductibles, limitations, and coinsurance provisions that it is very difficult to figure out before we buy into a policy how much we will have to pay under it. Each employer, each union, each group negotiates its own particular set of coverages, which vary from very minimal to very comprehensive. It depends on the employer's willingness, the union's interests, and many other factors. It also depends on the insurance company—what schedules of payment it uses, its policies and practices. Individual policies can be even more varied. Many Americans don't understand even the language of their insurance policy. Moreover, we don't really know how much illnesses cost and how much, say, twenty percent of a hospital and doctor's bill is going to amount to until we see it. All these factors work to prevent us from knowing how much our policy covers, how much will be left for us to pay, and whether we can afford to pay it. In other words, we aren't in a position to know whether our insurance coverage is adequate, or how vulnerable we are to financial disaster as a result of illness or injury.

Since we can't really judge for ourselves, most Americans accept the coverage offered by their employer, their union, or an organization to which they belong. The vast majority of Americans buy their health insurance as members of such group plans. Because their policies are very complicated, many people don't even read or try to understand them until they are sick and the hospital or doctor explains why there is so much left for them to pay. Most of the stories in this book involve such surprises, but most American families can tell stories of their own.

All these complications can make insurance coverages into dangerous traps which few of us can get through without being surprised—and in which many of us get badly hurt.

## People Who Fall into the Gaps

In far worse shape, however, are families who find they have no insurance at all when illness strikes. Many Americans in the course of their lives work for a number of different employers and come under different groups. As they move from group to group, or from group to private coverage, they may discover there are gaps—periods when they or a member of their family have no insurance at all.

We heard testimony from: Mrs. Rieger and Mrs. Moore, whose delivery costs were not covered by their employers' group plans because they took a maternity leave of absence from work; Mrs. Petrich, whose husband changed jobs during her pregnancy and found that his new employer's group insurance required an eleven-month waiting period before it paid maternity benefits; Mrs. Mapes, whose policy was canceled because she did not tell the insurance company her child had asthma—even though her doctor had not informed even her; and Mr. Cotton, who found upon leaving his job and losing his group coverage that he could not buy individual coverage for his wife because of some undiagnosed health problems she had been having, and ended up paying a bill of over $13,000, for brain surgery. Mr. Cotton's friends in the health insurance business advised him not to even apply for coverage for his wife. "You'll just be refused and it will spoil your chances of getting coverage later," they said.

There is also the case of Mr. Lyle Mattox of Chicago, a piano tuner, who faced the expenses of a heart attack without insurance because he was in a gap in coverage.

MR. MATTOX: At the time of my illness I had no private insurance, because they would not insure me.

SENATOR KENNEDY: Why not?

MR. MATTOX: In 1963 Prudential Insurance Company approached us about buying hospitalization and they sold it to my family, but they found out on examination that I suffered from high blood pressure, and that was the first time that I knew it. Then from then on I could not get hospitalization insurance.

SENATOR KENNEDY: You had health insurance, though, from 1949 to 1963, is that right? You were covered by a group plan?

MR. MATTOX: I was covered through—well, most of the war and up until 1962. I was covered by a group health insurance.

SENATOR KENNEDY: You have been covered from at least 1949, prior perhaps in terms of the war, but at least from 1949 to 1962 you were covered by a health insurance policy of your employer, which was the Music Department Store?

MR. MATTOX: Yes.

SENATOR KENNEDY: When you left that job, you lost your insurance, became a part-time worker at a music department and worked two hours a week short of qualifying for their group health policy, is that right?

MR. MATTOX: That is correct. That was at Roosevelt University, the Chicago Music College.

SENATOR KENNEDY: And then because of high blood pressure you were refused individual health insurance by several firms, is that right?

MR. MATTOX: By the beforementioned company, and also I was approached in the middle to late 1960s by Bankers Life Insurance Company, and they accepted my initial application knowing my blood-pressure condition, and the home office refused to ratify it and I did not receive it.

SENATOR KENNEDY: Why don't the insurance companies

want to insure you when you have got high blood pressure?

MR. MATTOX: They don't want to insure anybody unless it's a pretty sure bet. [Laughter.] . . .

SENATOR KENNEDY: Do you think the reason for this, in your case, was because of this high blood pressure?

MR. MATTOX: It is the only reason I was refused, yes.

Now, I have been approached recently by a company who says, "We will underwrite your hospitalization and medical costs despite the fact that you have had a coronary," but they will only underwrite three-fourths of the cost of any conditions relating to the coronary or to cardiovascular conditions, and the premiums will cost about thirty dollars a month. I have not yet heard from them as to whether my application was accepted.

Ironically, the gaps between insurance coverages frequently trap a man when he needs insurance most—when he has been laid off from his job, or is between jobs, or is trying to start his own business. If a member of his family gets sick or is injured during these times, he may be hit with high bills and no insurance right when he has little or no income. If a member of his family has a preexisting or recurring health problem, he may find he is faced with waiting periods in a new group policy and that it is impossible to get any individual coverage at all except by waiving benefits for costs connected with the preexisting problem. It is, of course, exactly this problem that he most needs coverage for, especially when he is between jobs.

## People Who Are Excluded from Insurance

Perhaps the people most hurt by our health insurance system are those with chronic diseases whom insurers simply refuse to insure, and families with low incomes who can't afford the costs they would have to pay for insurance. Not everyone who has a chronic disease is uninsured, nor are all low-income families without health insurance. If you are lucky enough to be able to join a group plan, you will be covered for whatever the plan covers and you will be able to buy into the plan at a reasonable cost. Unfortunately, joining a group, or even getting a job in a firm with group coverage, may prove difficult for those with chronic diseases. Some firms discriminate against such people for fear they will force up the group premium rate.

If you are disabled, self-employed, employed part time, or employed by a company without a group plan, or if for any of a dozen other reasons you cannot get into a group, you may find yourself trapped and unable to get insurance at all or only at a cost you can't afford. Individual coverage is very expensive; it costs much more than group coverage with comparable benefits. Many people who lose their group coverage are forced to settle for narrower coverages because they just can't afford the cost of good coverage under an individual policy.

Millions of Americans are excluded from coverage because of these high costs. According to the Department of Health, Education, and Welfare, only eight percent of American families with incomes of $10,000 or more a year lack hospital insurance, compared to twenty-two percent with incomes between $5,000 and $7,000, and forty-three percent between $3,000 and $5,000. Millions of Americans, especially in the middle and lower incomes, simply cannot afford health insurance.

We heard testimony from Miss Grace Bartlett in West Virginia how her Addison's disease had both disabled her and made it impossible for her to get insurance coverage; friends in the business had advised her for years not to even apply, because she would only be refused and would ruin her chances to get coverage later when she might get better; we heard from a physician in Des Moines how only twenty-two percent of the people in one low-income section of the city and forty-four percent in another low-income section had any insurance coverage; what with part-time employment, employment with companies that do not offer group coverage, and unemployment, many of the residents have no group coverage, and the cost of individual policies is too high for them to afford. Mr. Kenneth De Shetler, state insurance commission of Ohio, read the committee a number of letters from people who simply could not face the continuing rises in insurance premiums.

One of the most compelling stories we heard of a person's attempts to get health insurance coverage was told by a young woman student at a Southern university, whom we shall call Miss Thompson.

Miss Thompson: I was struck with polio in 1950, and it has required twenty years and twenty-five operations to come from a total paraplegic to what I am now, a partial paraplegic. . . .

The effect of all of this financially is what I'd like to talk about. . . . My parents were just starting in business when I was five, and they felt like it couldn't happen to them. Anything as catastrophic as polio couldn't happen to them. It was a question of either eating or paying insurance premiums, so they didn't have any insurance. My mother estimated that from the time I was five years old until I was nineteen they paid an outlay of approximately $65,000 for my illness alone. She received no help, with the exception of the Polio Foundation two times.

My parents' business was doing extremely well until about 1958, when there was a general business slump. . . . My father's business suffered reverses, and a lot of things happened in '65. Finally they put it in the hands of a receiver in July. The Sunday after that Friday he collapsed, and on Monday they said he had cancer. The following October he died. When he closed that plant it automatically canceled the health insurance for all employees and all members of the family, so he had no insurance. . . .

Now the American Medical Association and the Nixon Administration say if we go under private health insurance everything is going to be all right. I know from bitter experience this is not the case, because in my later life, when I was on my own, it has become me versus the insurance companies. I cannot get insurance, I can only come under group insurance plans, and I am being forced to enroll in the mass enrollment firms that advertise in the papers, and they are frauds of the worst kind, because I cannot get the insurance.

For instance, this summer I was going to school and I fell, necessitating surgery, back surgery, a spinal fusion. And the university's medical insurance, Zurich Insurance, refused to pay on the basis it was a preexisting condition, because preexisting conditions are not covered. It took a friend of mine who was a lawyer and nine months to force them to pay this. . . .

SENATOR KENNEDY: Why did the insurance company say that was a preexisting condition if it was after you fell? How did they know this?

MISS THOMPSON: Because I had had back trouble before. The surgeon's report definitely stated after he operated that it was because of a recent fall and two discs had been cracked and had not been calcified.

SENATOR KENNEDY: But the insurance company said it was preexisting?

MISS THOMPSON: Yes. . . . On most major claims I have had an attorney to force most insurance companies.

SENATOR KENNEDY: Who pays for those attorneys?

MISS THOMPSON: Well, I am very lucky in having some very nice friends who are attorneys, or else I could not afford it. . . .

Even if I have the group insurance, as I say, the problem of making them pay is tantamount to impossible. I had an ulcer attack, and I have yet to see what polio has to do with an ulcer, and they have used this as an excuse. I have riders, I have two insurance policies and both of them have riders on them—it says anything relating to the lower extremities is not covered.

SENATOR KENNEDY: Whom do you think the insurance companies represent if they don't represent the consumers?

MISS THOMPSON: They represent themselves. There are more ramifications to this than just health insurance. I have been denied three specific jobs because they will not cover me. They say to the company, "You keep down your risks, and we'll keep down your rates." They can go in and say your rates go up because last month you had five accidents, so the companies won't take that chance. . . . The reason I know this specifically is because of three job instances. People I became friendly with later have told me that they could not hire me because they had to keep down people with chronic illnesses. A vocational rehabilitation worker told a friend of mine that if I were a handicapped person and it was not visible he would not put it on an employment record, because right there they'd throw it in the trashcan. . . .

SENATOR KENNEDY: Let me ask you again, Miss Thompson, what do you estimate were the total medical bills just for yourself?

MISS THOMPSON: Sixty-five thousand dollars. . . .

SENATOR KENNEDY: Are you still paying any of that?

MISS THOMPSON: I am, and I will be for many, many years to come. . . . I have no idea what my medical expenses will be. They will be continuous until the day I die.


It seems clear that while the vast majority of Americans have health insurance of some kind, millions of Americans have far less insurance than is required to assure that they will not be bankrupted or forced to mortgage their future by health care bills. Millions more have no insurance at all. It also seems clear that most Americans do not know what they have and are surprised when they find out how little their insurance pays for. These problems, moreover, are worsening as health care costs skyrocket and as insurance premiums rise to keep pace with them.

### HEALTH INSURANCE: ITS FAILURE TO CONTROL COSTS AND IMPROVE QUALITY

Since 1960, physicians' charges have gone up twice as fast as the general rate of inflation in our country. Hospital charges have risen almost six times as fast. Moreover, the amount spent by the average American for health care each year has risen from just over $140 to $324. The Department of Health, Education, and Welfare has estimated that roughly sixty percent of this increase results from increases in prices and only forty percent from additional services to the people.

These increases occurred during a time of rapid expansion in the number of Americans enrolled in insurance programs. The increases indicate that the health insurance industry has failed so far to control costs.

### *Insurance Has Encouraged Unnecessary Hospital Care*

In fact, many experts feel that the design of insurance policies has actually helped to cause these increased costs. For example, policies have traditionally covered inpatient care in hospitals far more extensively than care in the doctor's office. As a result, insurance has given physicians an incentive to put patients into the hospital even when they might have done the tests or minor surgery in their office. That way the insurance covers it. Unfortunately, however, the same test or surgery when done in the hospital costs a great deal more. The cost comes back to the people in their part of the hospital bill and higher insurance premiums.

The few insurance programs which offer good coverage for care in the doctor's office show remarkable reductions in the number of times physicians send their patients to the hospital. In fact, some prepaid-group-practice plans cut in half the number of people sent to the hospital and significantly reduce the average number of days a person spends in the hospital once admitted. The result of lower hospital use is that the people in these plans pay less for their health care —or get more care for the same money.

Health insurance plans are only recently being modified to cover care in the doctor's office. Even today, most plans cover only certain items of care outside the hospital, and cover office visits in general only after large deductibles have been met.

*Insurance Hasn't Stopped Inefficiency*

In addition to encouraging care in the hospital rather than the physician's office, insurance has little power to prevent duplicate facilities from being built, duplicate services from being offered, many hospital services from closing down while patients lie idle in their rooms on weekends, or other inefficient and uneconomical operations from continuing and even expanding.

In some cases Blue Cross has challenged hospital costs and even refused to pay the costs of some hospitals when it felt they were way out of line. These challenges have been unsuccessful, however. In one widely publicized case in Philadelphia, the hospitals collected proxy votes and voted out of office the chairman and the treasurer of the Blue Cross board which took these actions, and forced the board to meet their costs. In the end, as the Ohio state insurance commissioner put it, Blue Cross saves all hospitals from insolvency, bad and good alike.

In a different approach to controlling costs, some of the larger insurers have established sophisticated computer systems to screen bills received from physicians and hospitals, in hopes of challenging and cutting out charges for duplicate, unnecessary, or fraudulent services. United Medical Services, Inc., Greater New York's Blue Shield plan, is acknowledged to be one of the best such plans in the country. Dr. Harold Safian, vice-president of that organization, testified concerning the aggressive and sophisticated efforts this organization has made to screen hospital and physician bills submitted to their plan. As a result of their efforts, the Blue Shield plan saved over $2 million in unwarranted charges. The plan, however, paid out $266 million in benefits. All of its efforts resulted in a saving of less than one percent of its payments.

In some cases when an insurer refuses payment of a bill, the patient ends up making up the difference. Dr. Safian assured our subcommittee that physicians who bill Medicare directly must accept the payment which Blue Shield, as the Medicare representative, offers. The president of Blue Shield plans in America offered similar assurances concerning all "participating physicians." That is, if a physician "participates" in the Blue Shield program, he must accept the payment which Blue Shield considers reasonable. However, many physicians bill Medicare patients directly for their services and leave it to the patient to collect from Medicare, and many physicians are not participating (roughly nine percent in the Washington, D.C., area). In these cases, the insurer's refusal to pay all or part of the bill can lead to the patient's making up the difference.

Moreover, most insurance companies do not use this "participating physician" concept and always require the patient to make up the difference between what insurance pays and what the hospital or the doctor charges. In these cases, if the insurer turns down a claim as unwarranted or pays only part of it, the policyholder is stuck with the difference. It is not the insurance company that must reach terms with the hospital or the doctor—the patient is left to do it for himself. If he is lucky he may have someone in his union to go to bat for him and negotiate a more reasonable charge. Mrs. Shirley Kronberg, with the New York Hotel Trades Council, described many such cases to us—cases in which she renegotiated hospital and physician charges for union members, sometimes after their insurance refused to pay.

Indeed, even though they have met with little or no success, Blue Cross and Blue Shield have occasionally tried to control costs. Most insurers have, in fact, been content to watch Blue Cross/Blue Shield battle unsuccessfully to control charges while they have simply raised premiums to cover the charges as they climbed relentlessly higher and higher. Even Blue Cross, however, far from controlling costs, may have contributed to inefficiencies. Its methods of payment do little to press a hospital or physician to greater efficiency. Many of the plans pay the hospitals their costs plus a percentage. If the hospital is inefficient and has high costs, these will be covered, plus the hospital gets a percentage of those costs in addition. Since the higher your costs are, the more that percentage amounts to, it is almost to your benefit to be inefficient.

Anyone who has been hospitalized over a weekend knows how things grind to a halt—except in emergencies—but meanwhile the daily room charge continues to be chalked up on the patient's bill. Many of us have gone from specialist to specialist and had identical tests or X rays repeated. Blue Cross/Blue Shield have done little to encourage greater efficiency in these or many other areas.

*Insurance Hasn't Improved Quality and Organization*

If the insurance industry efforts to control costs have failed, their effect on the organization and quality of care have been nonexistent. They have not caused the providers of care to offer better services to the people.

Some insurers claim that their reviews of hospital and physician charges help assure quality. They seem more effective, however, for protecting the insurance plan from fraud or intentional abuse. They do little to catch mistaken diagnoses, inappropriate treatment, and other day-to-day errors which distinguish good from bad medicine. In fact, even when the insurer identifies a hospital or a physician that gives consistently poor care or even makes fraudulent charges, the public does not hear of it. The patients will probably never know that their hospital or doctor is viewed with deep suspicion by a review board at the insurance plan. The insurer may turn the names of glaring cases over to the medical society for review. These cases are rare, and, from what I have been able to determine from medical-society witnesses, strong action by the society is even rarer. In any case, the people who use the services will very likely never find out that the services are suspect and be given an opportunity to choose another doctor or hospital.

With respect to improving the organization of health care and increasing the ease with which people can get health care, most insurers do nothing. Some of the larger companies and Blue Cross/Blue Shield describe special projects undertaken to test out prepaid group practices or other special arrangements. It seems that the bigger insurers are willing to adjust to new forms of health care if doctors, hospitals, and public go into them. However, it is not clear how these insurers are putting pressure on the providers to improve the way health care is organized, or how they are serving as representatives of the people to force the health system to better meet the people's needs.

In fact, almost all insurance plans are tied to the fee-for-service principle that pays each provider for each service to each patient. It is this principle that allows each physician and each hospital to set themselves up as independent businesses, with little incentive to organize with other physicians and hospitals to offer comprehensive and better-organized care. The insurers do not seem prepared to violate this principle—a true sacred cow in American medicine. Most insurers have not really even carefully studied alternative ways of paying for care, even though some progressive groups have for many years argued and demonstrated how prepaid group practice and other forms of financing care lead to better-organized health care.

Today the government is considering changes in Medicare and Medicaid laws, as well as new laws, to encourage physicians and hospitals to join together in organizations that provide a wide range of health services for a fixed amount per person per year. Most experts believe that physicians and hospitals who accept this challenge will be strongly motivated to give higher-quality, better-organized, and more comprehensive care to their enrollees. They will be motivated because the efficiencies possible in these arrangements will, in fact, allow such organizations to earn more income than other forms of practice.

The insurers might have pressed for such arrangements years ago when faced with skyrocketing costs and fragmented care. But they did not. They have not ever studied it thoroughly. They seem willing now to go along if the providers want it. That approach clearly is not serving as the people's representative to press for improvements in service to the people.

WHY PRIVATE HEALTH INSURANCE MUST FAIL

Why has the health insurance industry failed to set up adequate ways for Americans to share the risks and expenses of health care? Why has it failed to represent the people to control the cost of care and improve the way health care is organized? There are two basic reasons: misdirected competition among some 1,800 insurance organizations, and control of the insurance plans by the health providers.

## The Doctors and the Hospitals Control the Insurance Plans

Most of the 1,800 insurers in this country have never really tried to put pressure on physicians, hospitals, and other providers to hold down costs or change their manner of operation. Most of them simply ride with the tide, raising premiums to cover rising costs—and offering payment to providers in the classic fee-for-service manner, with no incentives for change. Those who have tried, such as Blue Cross/Blue Shield, have been beaten.

The reason Blue Cross/Blue Shield are beaten seems evident. The reason that the Philadelphia hospitals were able to stop the board members who wished to cut back on payments is that the hospitals effectively control Blue Cross managing boards. Hospital representatives are a majority or near majority on the boards of all seventy-four Blue Cross plans across the country. In fact, the Blue Cross trademark, a valuable asset in selling insurance, has been owned for years by the American Hospital Association and is granted by them to nonprofit insurance carriers. Action is only recently being taken to eliminate this obvious conflict of interest. Blue Cross negotiates and its board approves contracts for payment rates with each hospital participating in its plan. Thus hospital administrators, trustees, and others find themselves establishing policies governing their own or sister institutions. It seems highly improbable that such boards would put much pressure on hospitals to make any very demanding changes.

The situation with the Blue Shield plans is similar. The Blue Shield boards are dominated by physicians. The Blue Shield plan must be approved by the appropriate medical societies. Indeed, the fee schedules and administration for Blue

Shield plans is proposed by either the medical society or a committee in which physicians constitute a majority. The fee schedules are then approved by the physician-dominated boards.

The Blue Cross/Blue Shield arrangements seem better designed to protect the interests of the provider of health care than to protect the interests of the patient, the user of health care. It is hard to see how these boards could take a hard line with the providers, insisting on cost controls, efficiency, and better organization because the people want and need it. These boards have worried with minor changes and have worked to eliminate fraud in many cases, but they have not and never will take a hard-nosed stand on behalf of the people. They are set up to serve the providers, and they depend heavily on the providers' support. After all, if the physicians or the hospitals don't get what they want from Blue Shield or Blue Cross, they can simply refuse to do business with it. If hospitals and physicians stop accepting Blue Cross or Blue Shield coverage from their patients, it won't be long until the patients switch to other plans and Blue Cross and Blue Shield are forced out of the area. There are always other insurers willing to step in and advertise that hospitals and doctors accept their plan. In Massachusetts several years ago, a group of hospitals took exactly this position with Blue Cross and forced Blue Cross to meet their terms. In some areas of the country, physicians are considering setting up their own insurance carrier under a corporation controlled by the medical society, and freeing themselves completely from influence by Blue Shield and other carriers.

In the end, all of the insurance industry raises premiums to cover physician and hospital charges and goes along with the physicians and the hospitals on how the plan will operate.

In the end, the physicians and hospitals control the insurance carrier policies that affect them.

## Misdirected Competition Ruins Coverage

There is no competition among insurance companies to offer better-organized health care at lower costs. Only physicians, hospitals, and other providers can improve the organization of care and control costs. The insurance industry has not been able to move the providers to do these things. As a result, competition in the insurance industry has been directed—or, rather, misdirected—elsewhere. It is misdirected at designing newer, jazzier-sounding policies that people will think are valuable, isolating favored low-risk groups and offering them lower premiums, and screening out people whose health problems may cost money. Since all of the insurers face the same high hospital and physician charges, and none of the insurers can change these costs, they can compete only through the hard sell.

These are the very practices that have led to higher premiums for many Americans, to people's falling into the gaps between coverages, and to many Americans' being excluded from coverage altogether. It is difficult to see how competition in the insurance industry can lead to anything but *more* of these problems in years to come.

## Experience Rating

One indication of the stiff competition among insurers is "experience rating." A number of years ago health insurers realized that some groups of Americans are less likely to have high health care costs than others. Office workers, for example, have far fewer accidents than farmers. By limiting a health insurance plan to people in such a "safer" or low-risk group, the insurer can offer the same plan at a lower premium. The premiums can be lower simply because the company's experience indicates that it will pay fewer benefits to this group. By doing experience rating, insurance companies were able to go into low-risk groups, offer lower premiums than the existing insurer, and take away the business. Blue Cross and Blue Shield have been so threatened by competitors using this tactic that they also have begun experience rating.

At first glance, experience rating may seem like a good thing, especially to the people in the group with lower premiums. In the end, however, it is disastrous. Remember, the lower premium isn't offered because a group is getting health care at a lower cost, it is offered because this group has been singled out as low-risk on a statistical basis. The problem is that as the premiums go down for "safe" groups, the premiums go up for everyone else. As more and more "safe" groups are created, the premiums for "unsafe" groups—people with truly more hazardous jobs—go way up.

This basically contradicts the idea of pooling our payments in order to share the risks of getting ill or being injured. It amounts to keeping out of the pool those whose jobs make them a little more likely to cost the insurance company money. Its net result is to exclude more and more people from coverage because of its prohibitive cost. In fact, it excludes the people who are most likely to need it most.

In addition, experience rating results in even more pools being created. As different groups get rated individually, some elect to apply their savings to increased benefits, and others select a lower premium. As a result, there are more and more different policies at different costs in America, leading to more confusion and less understanding on the part of the people.

*Overpriced Policies*

Experience rating is only one form of competition, however. There are other, far more odious forms. There are insurance companies that write policies which sound glorious to the consumer. There are insurance salesmen who make them sound even better. Some of the companies that sell these policies, however, return to the policyholder only fifty percent or less of all they collect in premiums. With such companies, for every dollar a policyholder pays in premiums during his lifetime, he will get back an average of fifty cents or less in benefits. Of the other fifty cents, five cents may go for overhead, forty cents for sales commissions, and the rest for corporate profits. Blue Cross and Blue Shield and some of the larger group carriers do better in this regard, paying no sales commissions and keeping only six percent and eleven percent respectively for overhead. The federal Medicare program does even better, keeping only three cents of every dollar paid in by the American people for hospitalization and only ten cents of every dollar paid for medical benefits under Part B of Medicare.

Some companies build in exclusions, limitations, low-fee schedules and other techniques that boil down to the insurance company paying less and the patient paying more.

Many insurers who do not use these practices in the extreme do produce a wide variety of coverages and frequently put together special packages to sell a group policy. Each provision in each policy has a "cost" to the insurer which most buyers do not understand. A policy that ultimately returns only seventy-five cents on the dollar may look better to a buyer than one that pays ninety cents on the dollar.

In order to "sell" all these groups, hundreds, even thousands, of different policies are written, each with its own costs, limitations, exclusions, etc. It is no wonder that a wage earner seldom knows what health insurance he really has as he moves from job to job and from group policy to group policy, or into an individual policy. Experience rating, and competition to package benefits in a more attractive way serve to produce the gaps between coverages and the premium levels that exclude many Americans while keeping all Americans guessing about how adequate their insurance really is.

## Exclusions

The competition also forces insurers to protect themselves against those with possibly serious illnesses or chronic diseases. After all, if you allow people in with high blood pressure, for example, they are apt to have a heart attack and cost the company a lot of money. If you have many of these people, you would have to raise your premiums. If you raise them more than other insurers, you may lose business. Consequently, insurers are obliged to exclude coverage of the particular problem from the policy. One of the nation's leading health plans informed me in a recent letter that they must exclude people with such health problems lest their prices become uncompetitive with the experience-rated group policies in the community.

## The Moneychangers

Competition is usually a force that leads in part to better services at the same or less cost. Competition in the health insurance industry is not directed toward these ends, however. Competition among insurers *cannot* produce better services or lower costs from the physicians and the hospitals.

As a result, the industry has become basically moneychangers, taking the people's money and channeling it into the hospitals and the doctors. It cannot offer better care or better prices for care, nor can it influence the doctors and the hospitals. To sell its services, the industry has turned to high-powered marketing techniques that do not solve our problems but add to them immeasurably.

The insurers tie up insurance packages in different ribbons and paper and sell them to an uninformed public. Their drive for profit leads some to disguise a bad policy with fancy wrappings, preying on the needs of the uninformed for health care. The same drive leads many to look at their policyhold-ers' claims as "losses," as threats to their profit, rather than as opportunities to serve the people. This leads some to delay or deny payments until the policyholder sues or gives up.

Dr. Rashi Fein, a professor of medical economics at Har-vard Medical School, points out how a federal program, such as Social Security, can actually work to make sure people get their benefits. He said:

I don't believe that the interests of commercial health in-surers are necessarily consistent with the consumers' interests. I do believe that the interests of commercial health insurance —I do in part exclude Blue Cross—is in making money. I do not think that that is the interest of the Social Security Ad-ministration. I think the interests of the Social Security Administration are in protecting people, and I think there is a big difference between protecting people and making money.

Now, what does that mean in real life? It does not mean that insurance agents aren't nice guys, that they aren't kind, and that they aren't humane; they are nice guys, and they are kind, and they are humane, and so are physicians. Some of my best friends are physicians. [Laughter.] But they are caught up in a system that gives them rewards based on incentives which are not the incentives that ought to exist. So we have a processing of claims that makes things difficult for the individual. The Social Security Administration lends a hand and says, "You are eligible for benefits." I rather doubt that the commercial health insurance sector is going to go out of its way to remind people that they ought to collect on some claim. That is not their bag.

For their role as supersalesmen and moneychangers, the insurance companies take a big slice off the top of premium payments. For the 41.5 million Americans who paid $1.9 billion for individual health insurance with commercial carriers in 1969, the industry took 49.2 percent for "overhead" or profit. For the country as a whole, both group and private policies, these commercial carriers kept almost 17 percent, a total of $1.3 billion, of all the premiums paid to them. If the insurance carriers were helping bring about a better-organized health care system, one which offered better care and more reasonable costs, they would be worth this high cost. But for them to keep so much of the policyholders' money for serving merely as moneychangers is unacceptable. They simply are not earning it. I don't think policyholders know how many of their premium dollars go to pay for high salaries, advertising costs, and sales commissions rather than for health care. We cannot afford to let profiteers take the money which we need for health care.

## MY CONVICTION

*I believe that all Americans should contribute, according to their ability to pay, to a common fund which pays the cost of illness and injury in such a way that:*

*No one is confused or uncertain of his family coverage, but all are eligible for the same comprehensive benefits.*

*No one falls into gaps in coverage, but all are continually covered regardless of the nature of their employment.*

*No one is excluded from coverage because the cost is more than he can afford. Each man or family should pay premiums based on what he earns, but all men should receive the same comprehensive benefits.*

*I further believe Americans need an insurance program that will represent the people in negotiations with the providers of health care, and that can effectively influence physicians, hospitals and other providers to control costs, improve quality, and offer health care services in a way most acceptable to the people.*

*I believe that the providers of care need to be represented in the management of such a program in order to protect their interests and freedoms and to assure that the program's influence on providers is a matter of creative incentives and not coercion.*

*Only the government can operate such an insurance program in the best interests of all people. We can no longer afford the health insurance industry in America, and we should not waste public funds bailing it out.*

*There is no place for profit-making and competition for profits and high salaries in health insurance. These motives are at the root of the failure of the health insurance industry to offer adequate protection to Americans and to assure that the health care system is responsive to America's needs.*

*Even if we provided comprehensive government programs for the insurance industry's biggest problem cases—such as the poor, the disabled, the elderly, those with chronic diseases—and even if we wrote and enforced complex government regulations to reduce the gaps, exclusions, and other traps in private insurance, the insurance industry still could not bring about change in the health care system to control costs, improve quality, and offer health care services in a way most acceptable to the people. The industry would remain a moneychanger taking a percentage of our dollars for a dubious service.*

*The health insurance industry in its day has brought America a long way toward affording the cost of health care. But its day is past. I believe we should recruit the talented Americans who have operated this industry into the public service to staff a national health security program.*

CHAPTER IX

# Better Health Care at Lower Cost

# in Other Countries

IN the town of Kiruna, Sweden, which rests among snow-capped mountains in the Far North, I saw workers in the iron mines who were justly proud of the excellent system of health care provided for them and their families. Compare those mine workers, 150 miles above the Arctic Circle in Sweden, with the mine workers I saw in Kingwood, West Virginia, which is 150 miles from the halls of the nation's capital. Around Kingwood they can't get an ambulance in an emergency, and too few doctors are available even to fully use the hospital built in the town. We were struck by such contrasts everywhere we went in Europe. And gradually we began to realize how far we have gone in America in letting chance and the preferences of physicians determine who will get health care.

In Copenhagen I spoke with eighty-three-year-old Ingeborg Hinding, a resident of Massachusetts for twenty-four years before she returned to her native Denmark. She lives at a special center for the elderly in the city. It has been con-structed in a neighborhood where the elderly can have contact with the community and with young families. The apartments are designed with emphasis on the comfort, self-respect, and personal identity of the occupants. Residents are encouraged to furnish apartments with as many of their own belongings as possible. Health care is readily available to all the elderly. There are also facilities for recreation, and the products of occupational therapy are offered for sale to the public. Most of the proceeds go to the person who made the object, thereby providing meaningful employment for elderly people.

If Mrs. Hinding still lived in America, she might be a patient in one of the expensive, decrepit, isolated nursing homes in the center of Boston, a home run for profit, with inadequate health facilities and with almost complete isolation of the elderly from the surrounding community—truly a place to die a slow and lonely death. Denmark and other European countries provide a meaningful existence for their senior citizens, while the names of hundreds of elderly people in Dorchester, Massachusetts, are on long waiting lists for expensive, understaffed, and dilapidated nursing homes.

The fact is, the United States pays more per capita for health care than any other industrialized nation in the world, but it gets less health care. That is difficult to believe, but it is true. Every other advanced country assures good health care to all its people at a price they can afford, and spends a smaller portion of its wealth on health care than we do in America.

In order to see these other nations' health care first hand, I took the Senate Health Subcommittee on a two-week fact-finding mission to Europe and the Middle East in the summer of 1971. We visited Great Britain, Denmark, Sweden, and Israel. We talked at length with doctors, health officials, hospital administrators, insurance experts, teachers, students, government officials, and, of course, the man in the street.

While there were many differences among the health systems of the countries we visited, there were startling similarities which stood in stark contrast to our health care crisis in America. In each country, the people have decided to assure high-quality health care to everyone in their society as a matter of right. Granted, in each country the people continue to debate how to better organize their health care system and how to better pay for the services provided. This debate, however, takes place in the context of the decision that good health care should be available to everyone. Moreover, in the midst of their debate over how to improve their system, these countries have succeeded in assuring high-quality health care for their entire nation at lower cost. Each country we visited spends a smaller proportion of its gross national product on health care than does the United States. And, because of the rampant inflation of health care costs in America, the gap between us and them is widening.

In the United Kingdom the total expenditure for health services in 1970 was approximately 1.8 billion pounds. If this figure is converted to U.S. dollars and corrected for the disparity in population size and GNP between America and Britain, it is equivalent to $41 billion in the United States. America, by comparison, spent over $70 billion on health care in 1970. These figures strongly suggest that with reform of the delivery system in the United States, more health services of higher quality could be offered at less cost.

Most of us in America have been led to believe that health care is a disaster in Europe. We believe that the people in England and other countries cannot get health care and are unhappy with their systems. We believe that the people don't get to choose their doctors and that the government tells their doctors what to do. We believe that costs are out of control in Europe, worse than in America. We believe that the people are treated coldly by big organizations and have lost the doctor–patient relationship we've cherished in America.

From what I saw, these things are simply false. They are myths that we have been taught by those who fear they will lose their high incomes or their freedom of choice if America were to change its health care system.

The fact is, while most Americans are angry and frustrated about health care, most Englishmen, Danes, Swedes, and Israelis are not. The vast majority of citizens in the countries we visited describe their health care system with pride, and no major political party in these countries would dream of trying to repeal the system. Indeed, many of the people we talked to were horrified to learn that Americans have to worry about whether they can afford health care. The fact is also that while the federal government in America has fought organized medicine to pass such programs as Medicare and Medicaid, in Europe government and organized medicine have entered into a constructive partnership with which most physicians and hospitals are very satisfied.

The people of these countries, including the providers of health care, have good reason to be proud. They have begun to solve some of the problems that are causing the crisis in health care in America.

### EVERYONE CAN AFFORD HEALTH CARE

When you go to the doctor in Great Britain, you pay nothing. In Sweden you pay $1.40. If you need a prescription, it will cost a fraction of what we pay in America.

A common example shows the difference. Suppose a man and his wife catch the flu. Shortly thereafter their two children catch it also. After a lengthy siege, the husband's flu is complicated by bronchitis. This prompts the whole family to visit the doctor, hoping to lick the bug once and for all. When their turn comes, the doctor examines all four members of the family and writes prescriptions.

In America, the total cost of the doctor's services and the drugs will be almost sixty dollars. The family will have to pay this out of pocket, since their insurance even though it costs about $300 a year, covers only care in the hospital. Had that same family lived in Great Britain, there would have been no charge for the visit to the doctor, and the drugs would have cost $2.40. In Sweden the doctor's bill would have been $1.40 for each person, or a total of $5.60 for the family, and the drugs would have cost about eight dollars, half of their U.S. retail price—for a grand total of fourteen dollars. In Israel and Denmark the story is essentially the same.

Similarly, the patient pays little or nothing for hospitalization. In Sweden it costs a total of two dollars.

The reason these costs to the patient are so low is that the bills are paid by the governments, in most cases through a government insurance program. These programs are similar to our Medicare, but they cover everyone in the country regardless of age and regardless of income, employment status, or where one lives. Moreover, these programs are broader than our Medicare, covering almost all health care services.

The money to pay for these health programs is raised in European countries through taxes, and the governments use these tax revenues to pay physicians, hospitals, and other providers. And, as we have seen, the average family's taxes for comprehensive health care come to *less* than what the average American family currently pays for far less health care.

This system of health care means that the people do not

have to face the risk of financial ruin because of illness or injury, as we must in America.

This system means that every family and every doctor and hospital knows exactly what is covered and what is not—and they know that the cost of treatment will be paid. They do not have America's thousands of insurance packages with varying gaps, exclusions, deductibles, limitations, and coinsurance. No one falls into traps or gaps in coverage.

In these countries, a credit rating has nothing to do with health care. Whether a family gets care for their children depends only on need—never on whether the family can afford the care. In England, Denmark, Sweden, and Israel the people need not be cost-conscious—they can be health-conscious, and can get health care as they need it.

### HEALTH CARE IS AVAILABLE AND
### WELL ORGANIZED

In America we saw a beautiful hospital—in West Virginia —constructed with federal funds; we found an entire wing padlocked and empty. The hospital's occupancy rate was only fifty percent, because there are not enough doctors in the county to staff it.

In city after city in America, in areas like kidney transplants, open-heart surgery, neurosurgery, and radiation therapy, new and expensive units have been built primarily for reasons of prestige, not because of need, and they have been built at the expense of the public.

In Beverly Hills, California, there is a ratio of one doctor for every eighty residents; in Venice, California, fifteen miles and two hours away by public transportation, the ratio is one doctor for every 1,600 residents.

These illustrations dramatize the inefficient and disorganized system of American health care. By contrast, the nations of Europe have succeeded, at least partially, in solving these problems of organization and delivery.

In Sweden, for example, a system of physician and hospital regionalization exists. Each local district has a health officer, a general practitioner, and a small hospital staffed by internists, surgeons, pediatricians and radiologists. The local hospital works closely with the general practitioners and health stations in the area. More complex cases are referred to regional hospitals of intermediate size with facilities for long-term care, rehabilitation, and more sophisticated procedures.

Each district hospital is linked to a specific regional hospital. For still more sophisticated problems, each regional hospital is linked to one of the five university teaching centers in Sweden, where treatment is by referral only. All of these hospitals, physicians and health centers are linked together by an effective network of transportation services. They use ambulances, aircraft, trains and ships, and all the services are covered under the national health care benefits.

Similarly, Great Britain organizes its care in such a way as to assure care to everyone and to guarantee that patients can find their way through the health care system. The general-practitioner service provides virtually every man, woman, and child in Great Britain with a family physician who is able competently to manage over ninety-five percent of the illness and injury of his patient. For those who require special attention, the general practitioner is able to guide them into the complex maze of modern hospital medicine and into the hands of the appropriate hospital-based specialist. This general practitioner—everyone in Britain has one and can tell you his name—manages the patient's overall care.

This system is structured to allow a remarkable degree of freedom. Contrary to misleading myth, patients have free choice of a general practitioner within reasonable geographic limits, and, in turn, the general practitioner can exercise his right to accept or reject an application for a new patient to join his list.

As a matter of national policy, the general-practitioner service has received special attention from successive governments. Rightfully, general practitioners are considered the bedrock of the system, and access to specialists in the National Health Service can be gained only on referral from a general practitioner.

Because of the support of general practitioners, the specialist in Great Britain is free to concentrate on his narrow range of interests in patients already screened by another physician. For this reason, the British manage with fewer neurosurgeons serving their entire population of 50 million, than there are at present in the city of San Francisco with a population of less than one million. Similarly, two pediatricians suffice in Oxford, which had a 1968 population of 110,000, while New Haven, Connecticut, has about thirty pediatricians serving its 1970 population of approximately 134,000.

Another great achievement of the NHS has been in improving the geographic distribution of specialist services. These formerly were concentrated in the London area, in Edinburgh, and in other centers of medical excellence. The National Health Service has effected a radical change in the direction of a more rational distribution of these physicians.

Why can Norway, Sweden, and Finland provide district health officers for Lapland, when we can't find doctors to serve the poor of Appalachia or the migrants on the western slopes of the Rockies?

Why can the State of Israel place doctors in a family health care center to treat Arabs in the desert, when the ghettos of every major city in America cry out for medical attention.

Why can Britain train enough general practitioners to provide a family doctor for every person in the nation when we are losing general practitioners and have no doctor at all in many counties?

The answer is in the way we plan and use health resources. In Europe there is a mechanism for rational planning. The governments, together with the providers of health care, have assumed the responsibility for assuring that there are enough health care professionals, that they enter the specialties in which they are needed, and that they are distributed throughout the country according to need.

Sweden, for example, intends to double its number of physicians in the next decade, simply by increasing the number of medical students. Each student receives his education at public expense, and he receives a subsistence allowance in addition, independent of his income or social position. After medical school, a student may take his internship and residency in any hospital in Sweden. All hospitals in Sweden are accredited teaching hospitals, even in the most remote rural areas. We met Danish and Norwegian physicians in rural northern Sweden who had stayed to practice in these remote areas after doing their internship or residency training there.

In addition, the Board of Medicine in Stockholm determines the number of residency positions available in each specialty. It is thereby able to influence the number of specialists of each type. It influences the supply of general practitioners according to national needs.

In Beersheba, in the Negev Desert in Israel, construction has begun on a new medical school. The school is being built by the main insurance funds of the Israel Labor Federation. The primary purpose of the school will be to produce the general practitioners that Israel foresees will be needed in rural areas in the years ahead. In addition, the existence of the school will assure that rural physicians in the area have access to a center of academic excellence. The hope is that more physicians will be attracted to this rural area by the existence of the school. The school will offer quality health care to Arabs and Jews alike.

In addition, the Federation is working to assure that ambulatory care is available to every village and kibbutz in Israel. When the settlement is small, a physician may serve it and several other villages, with a nurse living on site to care for the ill between the physician's visits.

As a result of these efforts, these countries are solving health care problems similar to those in rural and inner-city America.


### HEALTH CARE FOR THE ELDERLY

The British health care system makes special efforts to meet the special needs of the elderly and those suffering from chronic illness. While the British seem dissatisfied with their present level of achievement, the standard of care provided for these patients and the imaginative innovations in their management stand in striking contrast to the common neglect which growing numbers of elderly and chronically ill face in the United States. The subcommittee saw first hand what can be done when professionals take the responsibility for seeking out those who need special services and for working together, as a team, to improve the quality of care and the quality of life for both the patients and their families.

In Britain I saw dynamic programs for care and rehabilitation for the elderly. The central objective is to maintain them as functioning members of society as long as possible in their homes rather than to incarcerate them in depressing custodial institutions.

This is done by careful initial assessment and frequent review of their needs. If they require institutional care, they are placed in pleasant but simple geriatric units where progressive nursing care is provided in conjunction with rehabilitation and training in self-help. This leads to early discharge. However, the patients are not thrown out to fend for themselves or to burden unduly the resources and patience of their families. Periodic reviews continue of the patients' needs and an impressive array of home services is provided. These include home nursing services, mental-health services, visiting physiotherapists and occupational therapists, home help services, meals-on-wheels, and a variety of other aids to maintain the patient as independently as possible for as long as possible in the home environment.

The more impressive of these programs clearly demonstrate effective coordination among various health care professionals and voluntary agencies. The latter include a wide range of activities such as "friendly visiting," social clubs, workshops, group holidays, day-care schools, assistance from nonprofit building societies, and Red Cross loan schemes. All these professionals and organizations focus themselves on the special needs of the elderly and chronically ill.

HEALTH CARE FOR CHILDREN

An example of what can be done by a nationally organized health program is Israel's mother and child health service.

The national government has set up programs that assure that every expectant woman and her newborn child receive insurance coverage for prenatal and postnatal care, and for delivery in a hospital. The program, in twenty years, has resulted in an increase from 4 percent to 84 percent in the number of non-Jewish women who deliver their children in hospitals. During the same period, the number of women who die in childbirth has been cut in half.

Under this program, children are extended preventive health services from birth to adolescence, with special programs of rehabilitation for children who are found to be handicapped.

Special health care centers under this program care for over 85 percent of the infant population. There are now few villages in Israel without such a center.

For a new nation to have moved so far in so short a time is a tribute to its people—as well as proof that with strong organization it is possible to rapidly change and improve health services to a nation.

THE DOCTORS ARE HEALERS

Contrary to myths which have been so freely circulated in the United States concerning Great Britain, British doctors were found to be largely supportive of their NHS and proud of both the equity of the system and the quality of care they provide within it. Through their democratically organized British Medical Association, which represents all factions and special interests among British doctors, they have a continuing and generally friendly working relationship with government.

At the same time, the doctors are obviously aware of their

dependence on the government for funds, and their relationship with government has not always been entirely happy. In the mid-1960s, for example, there was a brief interlude when many general practitioners were almost in open revolt over remuneration and other conditions of service. At one point, seventeen thousand had submitted their resignations from the NHS to their representatives in the BMA, to be used as a bargaining chip with the government. By negotiation, the crisis was averted and government moved a long way in the direction of meeting the demands of the general practitioners.

This example of open hostility between government and the medical profession is the sort of exception that proves the rule. Generally, the profession bears a cooperative and supportive attitude toward government. This attitude was expressed to me not only by leading representatives of the medical profession in the BMA but by many members of the rank and file. It is also noteworthy that the leadership of the Junior Hospital Doctors' Association, the only significant splinter group which is seeking to obtain separate negotiating rights for interns and residents, was generally supportive of the underlying principles of the NHS. In spite of the many real and serious grievances which these young specialists-in-training expressed regarding their conditions of service and career prospects, none expressed a desire to return to a free-market system of health care provision.

In Norway, I found that fee-for-service, private outpatient medicine coexists with state-operated facilities and state-salaried physicians. The Norwegian Medical Association, in cooperation with the Norwegian Health Insurance Board, sets what are called "normal" fees. A fee schedule is established and enforced by the Medical Association. The fee is closely linked to the amount the Health Insurance Board can reimburse the patient, which is currently about seventy-five percent. If the Health Insurance Board is unable to raise its reimbursement, the Medical Association will not raise its fees.

In Norway there are rarely serious disagreements, and physicians are well paid. They start from the basic principle that the patient should not suffer the financial consequences of his illness. For this simple reason, the doctors do not raise fees if the patient must bear the burden. Physicians who charge more than the agreed rates or who cheat the Health Insurance Board are expelled by the Medical Association. And ninety-five percent of all Norwegian physicians belong to that association. The physicians in Norway clearly feel a very strong commitment and obligation to their society—and they receive high income, prestige, and social position in return.

The situation we found in Israel was the same. The Israeli Medical Association has taken a leading position in advocating a uniform, compulsory national health insurance plan. Legislation is currently pending which would replace the many sickness funds with comprehensive national insurance. The Medical Association in Israel is leading the way to better health and national health insurance.

## CONCLUSIONS

*America can learn a great deal from the people of Europe about a society's need to assure good health care as a right. We can also learn a great deal from the successes and failures of health care in Europe and Israel. Their experience should enable us to design an even better health care system in America.*

*In many ways, America differs from all of the countries we visited. Our customs of free enterprise and limited government action must shape our health care system—as well as America's special needs and more extensive resources for offering health care. We must build an American health care system that preserves America's customs while assuring good health care to all our people at a price they can afford. It is selling America short to say it is impossible or that it will lead to "socialized medicine" or some other system that most Americans find distasteful. I believe we can build a uniquely American health care system that solves our health care crisis, while capturing other countries' success at offering better care at lower costs.*

CHAPTER X

# Good Health Care: A Right

# for All Americans

$E$ ACH of us risks our family's health and future in a gamble
that serious illness or injury will not strike us; or that if
it does, the health insurance we have will cover the costs; or
that if our insurance doesn't cover it all, we will be able to pay
the difference without hurting our finances too seriously. As
we have seen, millions of Americans lose this gamble trag-
ically. Americans are bankrupted and forced to sacrifice their
savings and family dreams on top of suffering through tragic
illness and injury. For many the cost is worse than the illness.
Moreover, all Americans are finding the gamble more and
more risky and expensive to make. It costs more to buy good
health insurance than we can afford, but it costs even more
to be ill or injured without insurance. Even when we buy
insurance, it is seldom good enough. The gaps, exclusions and
limitations in coverage leave us financially vulnerable in ways
we don't even realize until they happen.

We risk more than disastrous costs, however. We risk our
family's health itself. We bet that the physician or clinic we
choose has kept current with the latest in his field, reviews

his work with other specialists, and generally practices good medicine. We bet that we can get to our family doctor when we need him, and from there to the specialist, to the laboratory, to the hospital, to the nursing home, to the drugstore, and so on as necessary. We bet that there will be a place for us or someone to help us at each place, and someone who pulls together the work of all these people and institutions to diagnose and treat our illness or injury.

As we have seen, millions of Americans lose on these gambles also. Americans are given widely varying quality of care. Many of us are subjected to unnecessary surgery or treatment, while some suffer long and needlessly because the physician is simply wrong. Many others of us spend anguished hours waiting for care, trying to get help after hours or out of town, or fighting our way from one specialist to another and from doctor to laboratory to hospital, repeating tests, hearing conflicting opinions, and losing hours of work.

Americans have relied on health insurance companies and on the doctors, dentists, hospitals and other providers to assure us good care at an affordable cost. The fact is that the health insurance industry assures us only that it will raise premiums enough to cover skyrocketing hospital and doctor charges and still assure its own high salaries, profits, and sales commissions. It has failed to adequately protect Americans from disastrous health care costs by spreading the cost and risk among all Americans. It has also failed to use the enormous amount of money it pays hospitals and doctors (over $15 billion in 1969) to press those providers to offer health care more economically and in ways, at times, and in places suited to the need of the millions of Americans who pay billions of dollars in health insurance premiums. The insurance industry pays for the health care, however poorly the care is organized and offered.

Nor have the hospitals, the doctors and other providers assured us good care at affordable costs. Care is offered by most providers in ways, at times, and in places most convenient to them, and most likely to assure them a good life at a high income. That is why you can't get a doctor in the middle of the night. That is one of the reasons costs are so high. Nor do providers do enough to guarantee quality. Most medical and other professional societies do little to insure that their members keep current in their field, subject their work to the review of their peers, or otherwise assure the quality of the health care they offer. Even when these societies (or insurance companies) know who the bad hospitals, doctors, or dentists are, they won't tell the people, and they rarely take effective action of their own. Unlike other American businesses, health care providers do not feel the competition and pressures from the people who buy services that assure that the services are offered in a way and at a price most attractive to the people.

It does not make sense that something Americans value as deeply as good health care at an affordable cost should hinge on our gambles on the insurance industry, whose interest is profit and not good protection for our people. Nor can we gamble completely on providers, whose own income and life style are at stake. It is tragic that Americans continue to make such gambles with health care when we are capable of doing more.

It is perhaps even more tragic that some Americans don't even have a chance to make this gamble. They are all but shut out from good care because their incomes are too low to buy insurance or to pay for care, because their age or disability makes them unable to get through the fragmented system, or because they live in an area where there is little or no care available. These Americans must drive long distances, or wait six to eight hours in the waiting rooms of public hospitals, or face possible insult from physicians and hospitals that refuse them treatment. It is callous beyond belief that we have created a health care system so unwilling and unable to respond to people with special needs that it almost shuts out Americans who are disadvantaged by age, disability, low income, or even by the fact that they live in rural areas.

No child should grow up in America with limbs still twisted because of the lack of health care.

No American should be forced by unnecessary bad health to live in poverty and watch his family grow up without the good health care that might improve their chance for a better life.

No elderly or disabled American should be forced to suffer alone because he is no longer strong enough or wealthy enough to fight his way through the system.

No American should be deprived of good care because he must travel so far or wait so long to get it that it is practical only in emergencies or when an illness has become serious.

Indeed, the way health care is offered and paid for in America today, none of us has any real assurance that he or his family can get good health care at a price he can afford. All of us risk, to some extent, our family's health and future in a gamble we need not make. We have the knowledge and the wealth in our nation to assure ourselves and every American that good health care is available to him and his family at a price he can afford. Other nations have succeeded in assuring good health care to their people and have proven that it can be done at reasonable costs. Why not assure such care to every American? I believe we should assure good health care to ourselves, to our families, and to everyone living in this country.

Good sense and responsibility to our own deepest values demand that we make this assurance. The opportunity for health is too important to our opportunity for a full life to run the risks of our present system of paying for health care through insurance companies and leaving the providers free to offer health care as they choose. I believe the federal government should take actions on our behalf to assure that every American has good health insurance coverage, and to assure that the wants and needs of the people are a more compelling influence in offering health care than is the convenience and profit of the providers. The federal government should simultaneously take actions to improve the efficiency, the organization, the quality, and the capacity of our health care system, in order to make sure the health care system is equipped to offer every American the good comprehensive health care that his new comprehensive health insurance coverage would enable him to afford.

There are a variety of proposals before Congress addressing one or more of the problems of assuring good health care to all Americans. I believe that only one of these proposals, however, will make the fundamental improvements required in both insurance and the organization and delivery of health care. That is the Health Security Act. I believe this bill will make these changes and at the same time protect the rights of the providers and open to them new opportunities for professional growth.

THE HEALTH SECURITY PROGRAM

Under the Health Security Program, the federal government would become the health insurance carrier for the entire nation. Rather than relying on the insurance industry to provide good health insurance coverage, Americans, by passing this bill, would ask their federal government to provide this insurance. The bill also would call on the federal government, as insurance agent for the nation, to set up controls and incentives for dentists, hospitals and other providers to assure that the health care offered to all Americans is of high quality, of reasonable cost, and offered in ways, at times, and in places responsive to the needs of the people. In addition, the program would set aside a portion of all the funds the government would spend on health care in a Health Resources Development Fund to educate the people, build the facilities, and organize the new types of services needed to offer good care to all Americans. In short, the program calls on the federal government to make sure that every American can pay for health care, that every American has good health care offered to him in ways suited to his needs, and that enough providers, facilities, and equipment are available to do the job.

## THE PROGRAM WOULD GIVE THE BEST HEALTH INSURANCE IN THE WORLD TO ALL AMERICANS

The government would provide identical insurance coverage to all Americans for all essential health care. It would be as if the federal government issued a group insurance plan where every resident of the United States was a member. Unlike the present system, you would get the same health care coverage regardless of where you work, what insurance company your policy is with, what previous illnesses you have had, how old you are, or how much you earn in income. No one would be excluded. Every American would have a comprehensive policy with the federal government from the moment he is born until the day he dies.

There would be no deductibles, no coinsurance, and no copayment of any kind—that is, you would not have to pay the first fifty or a hundred dollars each year, nor would you have to pay part of anything more than that. Nor could you use up your insurance. There would be no upper limits on how much the insurance would pay. The insurance would pay for as much care as needed to get you well. The program would pay for eyeglasses, hearing aids, and artificial limbs, even for crutches and wheelchairs.

Moreover, the insurance would pay for the health care you receive whether it is in the hospital, in the doctor's office, at home, or in a nursing home. It would cover:

- All hospital care.
- All physician's care.
- All dental care (starting with children through age fifteen).
- Home health care.
- Psychiatric care—unlimited when given in a "comprehensive health service organization," otherwise limited to forty-five days a year in hospital and twenty psychiatric consultations.
- Laboratory tests.
- Prescription drugs for the chronically ill, and for everyone treated in a comprehensive health service organization.
- Medical care in skilled nursing homes—limited to 120 days a year.

The intent is to cover all basic medical services. In order to get time to train and equip more dentists to meet the increased demand expected for dental services, dental coverage is phased in, starting with children who are age fifteen or less when the law takes effect. Once covered, however, a person remains covered throughout his life, so that eventually everyone will be covered.

The limitation on psychiatric care is intended to move psychiatrists and other professionals to treat patients on an outpatient basis in the framework of a comprehensive health or mental-health center. In such a setting, the benefits are unlimited.

The bill proposes to pay for *medical* care in nursing homes, but not custodial care. The limit of 120 days is viewed as a limit beyond which a person seldom needs to be kept in a nursing home for medical reasons.

With these exceptions aimed at phasing in the program or changing the way health care is offered, the program covers all medical care to all Americans without limit.

THE PROGRAM WOULD OFFER AMERICANS MORE CARE
AT LESS COST

In the early years of the program the average American family would end up paying the same amount for comprehensive health care under the Health Security Program as they would pay for less comprehensive care without the program.

The incredible fact is that even estimates of the cost of the Health Security Act by its opponents acknowledge that the amount our nation would spend on health care under this act would be only eight percent over the amount we would spend on health care just as it is today. In fact, distinguished supporters of the act insist that the same amount would be spent with the act as without it in its initial years.

Moreover, the real payoff in costs under the act would be

in the future. Only the Health Security Act incorporates strong cost controls and incentives for efficiency aimed at slowing skyrocketing health care costs. Without this act, costs will continue to rise as at present. Indeed, other national health insurance proposals may well speed these cost increases by feeding more money into the existing system while taking little or no action to correct its glaring inefficiencies.

The Health Security Act would bring rising costs under control. Consequently, in later years the act would provide Americans more health care at far lower costs than they would pay without the act.

## Budgeting to Control Costs

The Health Security Act would place the providers of health care on a strict budget. Hospitals and other institutions would prepare budgets to cover their operation in the coming year. After local health planners reviewed the budget to eliminate unnecessary costs, such as duplicate services among hospitals in the same community, the local Health Security office would negotiate a final budget which would determine the federal government's payment to the hospital. These budgets would be designed to promote expansion in needed services, such as outpatient clinics, but curtailment or conversion of excess facilities which add to overhead costs. Once the budget is set, the hospital's costs must be kept within it.

Likewise, the federal government would establish a budget for payment of physicians, dentists, and other providers. The budget would be large enough to cover all payments to these physicians for services to their patients, would allow a controlled increase in physicians' incomes to match increased costs of living, and would be adjusted to reflect increased services.

*Incentives for Efficiency and Lower Costs*

In addition to this tightly controlled budget process, the Health Security Program offers powerful incentives for more efficient health care.

Since the plan covers all forms of care, whether given in the hospital or in the doctor's office, there would no longer be an incentive to hospitalize patients in order to get insurance coverage. Moreover, since the hospital is paid on the basis of an annual budget and not on the basis of how many beds are filled, the hospital would feel less pressure to fill its beds in order to meet its expenses. Pressures such as these are widely acknowledged to result in many people being unnecessarily hospitalized or kept in the hospital longer than necessary. Organizations such as the Kaiser-Permanente Group Health Plan find that when these pressures are removed the number of hospitalizations is cut over fifty percent. Since hospital care is by far the most expensive form of health care, less hospitalization results in dollars saved for use in providing more health care in the doctor's office or the clinic.

In addition, the program offers financial incentives to physicians and hospitals to form comprehensive health service organizations. These are prepaid group practice organizations which offer all essential health care services for a fixed amount per person per year. Such organizations not only reduce the amount of hospitalization for their patients, but also manage to care for many more people than the same physicians can treat practicing on their own. They do this by organizing physicians of various specialties under one roof with a common supporting staff, laboratory, and other services, and by emphasizing preventive care which aims at keeping patients healthy and at diagnosing illness early, when it can be treated at the least possible cost and the least possible suffering. Can you believe that some such organizations send reminders to their patients that it is time for a checkup? Even though they are paid no more for such services, they offer them in the belief that they will pay off in the long run in less illness and lower cost of treatment. While other national health insurance bills encourage formation of comprehensive health service organizations (the President's bill calls them "health maintenance organizations"), only the Health Security Program provides the framework of comprehensive national health insurance and provides generous start-up support necessary for these organizations to be offered as a choice for all Americans of all incomes.

The program also contains a variety of other provisions aimed at increasing efficiency. It pays for home health care so that, wherever possible, people may be treated by a visiting nurse in their homes rather than being admitted to the more costly nursing home or hospital. It offers incentives for nursing homes and hospitals to form affiliations which encourage transfer of patients from the hospital to the less expensive nursing home at the point in their recovery where intensive medical surveillance or treatment is no longer necessary. Controls are established also to assure that excessively costly drugs and medical devices are not used when less expensive ones are equally good.

All of these and other provisions of the bill aim at encouraging more health care at less cost, and would result in the American taxpayer's getting more care for his dollar than in the present system. No other national health insurance program in Congress contains the wide range of carefully thought-out incentives for efficiency found in the Health Security Program.

THE PROGRAM WOULD ASK EVERY AMERICAN TO PAY
BASED ON WHAT HE COULD AFFORD

Instead of paying private insurance companies, doctors, dentists, hospitals, laboratories, and others for health care, Americans would pay the federal government. They would pay for their insurance through a one percent payroll tax (2.5 percent for self-employed) and through their income taxes. The man who earns more would pay more, and the man who earns less would pay less. But all would get the same benefits. Employers would pay a tax of 3.5 percent on their payrolls, but they would be relieved of private health insurance premiums.

From these funds the government would pay directly the doctors, the hospitals, and other providers. Since both the patient and the doctor know the bill will be paid, money will no longer be a consideration for a patient seeking any health service. Americans will no longer be discouraged from seeking needed care because they can't afford it, nor will pressured doctors and hospitals have to worry about whether a patient can pay or whether his insurance will cover the care. No hospital will any longer have "charity" patients, because every American will be eligible for care at any hospital or from any doctor he chooses, and the same fee will be paid regardless of the patient's income. In this situation, both patient and physician can afford to be health-conscious rather than cost-conscious.

THE PROGRAM ASSURES QUALITY OF CARE

As a condition for receiving payments for services from the federal government, hospitals, physicians, and other providers would have to meet national standards which would assure that institutions maintain the best possible facilities and have available adequate trained staff; that physicians, dentists, and others are current with the latest in their specialty or field; that physicians do not perform surgery for which they are not qualified; and that major surgery or specialized services are performed only after review of the need for the services by a physician in general or family practice, and in some cases by another specialist as well. The program also requires that drugs and medical devices be prescribed from lists established by specialists to indicate what drugs are safest and most effective for various purposes.

Providers who do not meet these standards will be excluded from the plan. Patients who feel they have been mistreated by the provider will be able to lodge complaints with the administrators of the Health Security Program.

Perhaps most important of all, the program offers strong incentives to physicians to organize prepaid group practices and other forms of practice in which they have a continuing need and opportunity to review the records of their fellow physicians' work and consult with them about it.

### THE PROGRAM ENABLES THE HEALTH CARE SYSTEM TO SEEK OUT THOSE WHO NEED CARE

The program will extend special services to Americans who are disabled or elderly, who are unable or too poor to get transportation, or who live in the country or the inner city where doctors will not presently go.

For the elderly, the disabled, and others with similar problems, the program offers home health care and emergency transportation to the doctor or the hospital. It will even pay for nonemergency transportation when getting to the doctor or the hospital is a problem. In addition, the program's Health Resources Development Fund will support projects designed to reach out to meet the special needs of these and other Americans.

Physicians, dentists, hospitals, and other providers would be attracted into shortage areas by the opportunity for practicing modern health care in these areas at an income comparable to other parts of the country—and by economic pressures. By making every American equally eligible for health care paid for by the federal government, the Health Security Program would make it possible for a physician, a dentist, or any other provider to make a good income even if he practices among the poor. This fact in itself would enable hospitals and individual doctors to open their doors to people and reach out into communities that they presently cannot afford to serve. In addition, in the process of setting up budgets over the years for regions and service areas across the country, the health service planners would move toward equal sharing of funds and facilities among all areas of the country. This would mean that some areas of the country that currently spend unusually large amounts on health care, that have the most extensive facilities, and that receive the largest number of services would be held even, while funds to purchase care and new facilities will be diverted into areas that are currently short of services. In the future there would be more and more money to be made in shortage areas by providers while the competition for income in highly served areas would be increasingly stiff.

At the same time that financial resources to buy care are being diverted into shortage areas, the program will make funds available to health profession schools to turn out more physicians, dentists, and other professionals. Funds will also be available to institutions to develop and implement satellite clinics, computer-supported communication systems, and other mechanisms designed to enable physicians to offer the latest in health care in these shortage areas and to make practice in these areas more attractive professionally.

### THE PROGRAM ORGANIZES OUR HEALTH CARE

The comprehensive health service organization would offer all essential health services to its enrollees, frequently in the same building or complex. In all cases the patients' treatment would be coordinated by the organization, and referrals would be simplified to the greatest extent possible. The aim of the program is to establish enough such organizations to makes this form of health care available to all Americans who want it.

For those who want and need assistance in finding their way through the current maze of health services, the comprehensive health service organization would be a valuable opportunity.

Moreover, by encouraging affiliations between health care institutions, and by requiring coordinated planning of what facilities are built and where, all Americans will benefit from better balanced services.

As for fragmentation of insurance plans, it will cease. Medicare, Medicaid and other programs will be absorbed in this more comprehensive plan, and thousands of private insurance plans will cease to exist.

THE PROGRAM FREES THE HOSPITAL AND THE PHYSICIAN
TO BE HEALERS BUT PRESERVES THEIR INDEPENDENCE
AND FREEDOM OF CHOICE

Providers would be freed of the burden of collecting from patients and from hundreds of insurance companies, freed of concern over whether special services to people with special needs can be afforded, and offered the resources to start new forms of practice or the opportunity to maintain their practice as in the past.

Physicians, dentists, and other providers can select payment on a fee-for-service basis or on the basis of a fixed amount per enrolled patient per year. They can choose solo practice, they can join a group, or they can work under salary, whichever they prefer. Clearly, different patterns of payment and practice are appropriate to different situations, different parts of the country, and different individuals.

Moreover, the people will have freedom of choice over the physician and the type of practice they prefer. Indeed, it is the essence of the plan that a choice of physicians and various forms of practice be available to the people in order that their preferences can be expressed.

There will, of course, be pressures on providers to control costs, to offer needed services, to insure quality of care, and otherwise meet the health needs of the people. While the program anticipates no decrease in providers' income, it will place financial pressures on providers to keep costs down and to improve efficiency.

These pressures, however, will be no greater than those felt by any business in America attempting to offer attractive services at competitive rates. These pressures have been constructive generally in America and they can be constructive for health care.

Indeed, on the other side of these pressures is the opportunity for providers as entrepreneurs to choose from a wider set of options for practice than has been available to them in the past—and the opportunity for those with the imagination and the will to obtain the financial resources needed to offer new forms of services and new types of practice that extend their skills and capacity as healers.

## THE PROGRAM WILL PLAN AND CREATE THE CAPACITY TO OFFER GOOD HEALTH SERVICES TO ALL AMERICANS

A unique feature of the Health Security Program is its planning for all areas and regions of the country and its establishment of a special fund to build the facilities and educate the personnel needed to provide good health care.

The Health Resources Development Fund, consisting of several billion dollars a year, will be used for these purposes, as well as to start up comprehensive health service organizations; set up programs of continuing education for providers; establish new forms of health services appropriate to rural and inner-city areas and to special groups such as the elderly and the disabled; and to support any new, innovative or special services by which providers can better meet the health needs of the people.

In order to allow time to create capacity to offer more health care, the program puts this Health Resources Development Fund into operation two years before the rest of the health insurance plan takes effect. Between improvements in the efficiency of existing resources and creation of new resources, the nation will be able to offer more services to more people under the Health Security Program than it could ever offer otherwise.

THE HEALTH SECURITY PROGRAM WOULD BELONG
TO THE PEOPLE

The program would not be run by the federal government for itself or by the providers for themselves. It would be run by the federal government for the people, and the people would be given every opportunity to shape the program to meet their needs.

At national, regional, and local levels, consumers would be in a majority on councils that would advise the government on how the health plans should be run. State and local planning agencies would advise on the needs for various services in their areas. Consumer-based community agencies would be encouraged to set up and manage their own comprehensive health service organizations, and all such organizations would be obliged to give consumers a strong say in how they offer services.

Ultimately, the people could influence their Senators, Congressmen, and President by their votes and could hold them accountable for how the program is run.

The biggest single reason, perhaps, for the problems in our health care system is that the people have had no way to influence when, where and how health care is offered and what it will cost. The Health Security Program aims at giving the people this influence.

## CONCLUSION

*We have a choice of conscience to make in America. It is a choice of whether we will assure each other and all Americans good health care at a cost they can afford. The pages of this book are filled with the tragic stories of people who have been hurt because we do not make this assurance. We can put an end to such stories, and I believe we should. I urge Americans to search their hearts to choose and to make their choice known. To take so major a step the government needs your support.*